Grammar and Thinking

A Study of the Working Conceptions in Syntax

By

Alfred Dwight Sheffield

Formerly of the Staff of Webster's New International Dictionary

G. P. Putnam's Sons
New York and London
The Knickerbocker Press
1912

The Knickerbocker Press, New York

Grammar, philosophically studied, is akin to the deepest metaphysics, because in revealing the constitution of speech it reveals the constitution of thought, and the hierarchy of those categories by which we conceive the world.

GEORGE SANTAYANA: *The Sense of Beauty*, p. 169.

It cannot be a matter of indifference to us to note, above the seeming chance that governs the words and forms of language, the appearance of laws corresponding in each case to an advance of the mind.

MICHEL BRÉAL: *Semantics*, xxvi.

PREFACE

THE advance of linguistics has left students of grammar at a somewhat disconcerting pass. Their subject, although centuries old in the schools, attained critical standing as a science but yesterday, so that they find themselves working with a tradition and terminology no longer abreast of the facts. Tradition, for example, looks to the word as their unit of analysis, and to the written page for the criteria of a word. It thus sets *homme(s)* over against *homin-em*, *homin-ēs* as a bare root-word, forgetting that actual talk uses in *l'homme*, *un homme*, *des hommes* what are practically not added words but flectional prefixes; it takes *il vient* as '*he* comes,' forgetting that context, precisely as with *ven-it*, may show the subject to be not 'he' but 'it' or a following clause; and it then interprets as a lack of flection in the language what means rather (as one writer observes) a lack of flexibility in the grammarian. Their terminology, pulled about between spasmodic efforts to fit inherited names to new conceptions of fact, has become a Babel in which even so staple a construction as *he is good* can be found described in nine different ways. The situation has indeed called out, both here and abroad, a propaganda of reform; and a British Joint Committee has already offered a scheme of harmonised nomenclature. But the discussions upon this movement make it increasingly clear that questions of terminology must be approached through a fresh appraisal of the notions that our terms presuppose. Such an appraisal this little book aims to formulate. I address it to teachers and serious learners in both classical and modern language-study, who would follow the ideas they work with into their background of psychology and logic.

My direct obligations in the text I have marked with foot-notes; but to Wundt's *Völkerpsychologie* I owe more than can appear in express citations, for I derived from its study an orienting in the whole field. Of other authorities I should mention gratefully Paul's *Prinzipien der Sprachgeschichte*, E. P. Morris's *Principles and Methods in Latin Syntax*, the chapter on "Semantic Change" in Professor Oertel's *Lectures on the Study of Language*, and that on "Speech and Signification" in Professor Santayana's *Reason in Art*. Professor Hartley B. Alexander and Dr. Horace M. Kallen have generously given me expert criticism upon passages in the manuscript where, as a layman in philosophy, I must otherwise have lacked assurance. Indeed, what seems distinctive in my account of sentence-*value* was prompted by Dr. Kallen's astute comments.

A. D. S.

CAMBRIDGE, MASS.,
December, 1911.

CONTENTS

Grammar and Thinking

Grammar and Thinking

I. THE SCOPE OF GRAMMAR

Grammar as a Study of Thinking. Old-fashioned definitions of grammar term it either "the science of language" or "the art of speaking and writing correctly." Both formulas are too loose, although a General Grammar, such as the first would offer, has been achieved, treating not of any one language but of formative principles that enter into all. Even the second, which plainly has in view not language but *a* language, would take in more features of speech than fall to the grammatical province. Mr. Yellowplush's remark that his '*ma rapt* up his *buth* in a *mistry*' is not "correct" speech, nor was Li Hung Chang's greeting to General Grant as 'a man *made to order*' (i.e., born to command); but their words are quite unimpeachable in grammar. Words are the subject-matter also of dictionary and rhetoric, and concern grammar only in the forms they take, and the ways they combine, for sentence-structure. Present grammars, therefore, limit their scope more accurately to the sentence, "the unit of discourse expressing a thought." But at this point our text-books are apt to grow vague. 'Word,' 'sentence,' 'thought'—these familiar terms, once we are pressed for a precise account of them, are found to involve distinctions which their very familiarity has prevented us from thinking out. It is certainly part of the concern of grammar to improve on the hazy popular notions of these things, and its failure to do so is what has lowered the subject in educational repute. The grammar of foreign speech, of course, can get on merely as an account of novel forms to be learned, but the grammar of one's mother tongue must justify itself as a discipline, imparting insight into the nature of the language-medium. No result so fruitful can now be claimed for school work in English. Its teachers and text-book makers who really come to close quarters with idiom in free play are bound to fetch up short with its uncritical nomenclature; while those in the elementary grades, keeping to "copy-book" sentences in which their definitions are valid, draw the reproach of merely "enterlacing a plaine matter with quiddities and ink-pot termes." In fact, the grammar taught in our schools lies under a stigma as unprogressive. It can hardly be said to offer the elements of present linguistic science, re-grounded as this has been within the past thirty years. What is here urged in remedy is that its account of the facts of speech should first of all reflect the ascertained facts of conceptual thinking.

Even school grammars now profit by the work of phonetics with the vocal stuff of speech. But speech itself makes part of the stuff of thought —the ideas which float in trains through one's waking life. An idea shows two elements: (1) a mental image, which conveys (2) a meaning. Thus in thinking of Rome one may have a faint visual wraith of the Forum. This mental picture, of course, is not the idea itself. One's idea of Rome is a complex and cumulative resultant of many experiences, such as reading Tacitus and Mommsen, seeing the aqueduct at Nîmes, hearing the Latin mass, etc. But the mental picture is what makes the meaning present to one's mind. Some image, in fact, must come to mind, if one is to think an idea at all.[1] The image need not be

[1] Strictly speaking, the image is often both a part of the meaning and a symbol for the rest of it. As part, it gives one of the meaning's details; as symbol, it turns attention towards details that are significant for the impelling interest. The image, that is, does not picture significant details but gives a clue to them. In fact, even as symbol the image can be distinctly made out only when we pause to reflect on what we mean. As my former colleague, Professor Alexander, comments: "The onflow of actual thinking outruns its own symbolism. Images become reduced from hieroglyphic to cursive form, in which all their sensuous likeness gets lost, so that we think algebraically or even in terms of mere 'bearings' and 'trends' of thought-masses, not analytically imaged at all."

visual; it may be a like shadowy revival of a sound, or of a feeling of touch or muscular effort. For many ideas, especially for the more abstract or general ones, the reinstating image is simply that of the word: either its muscular articulation, its sound, or both. Words, therefore, are what make the higher reaches of thought possible. With a gesture-language we should have visual images for *weave*, *model*, *whittle out*, but we should be put to it to suggest the general notion *make*. People of undeveloped speech can hardly think such ideas as 'action,' 'change,' 'organism,' 'tendency.'

The *meaning* of an idea is its fixed reference to some objective identity. The same image may in different contexts answer to different meanings. In one train of thought the image of a heap of goods might arise in the idea 'wealth,' in another it might mean 'commerce.' Meaning alone passes between mind and mind. If I say, '*a triangle inscribed in a circle*,' my hearer and I will forthwith think the same meanings, but we will have as mental images neither triangles of the same shape, nor circles of the same size. This loose fit between image and meaning follows from the fact that as compared with a first-hand "percept" an idea-image is faint and sketchy. It lacks the filling-in of sharp and distinctive detail given by an object of sense-experience. "But indeterminateness in the image involves indeterminateness in the meaning, in so far as expression of the meaning depends merely on the presence of the image without being otherwise defined and developed."[1] Simply by lacking particularity, therefore, an idea may be said to involve in itself some degree of generalising. Its actual degree of generality depends on how it is developed within a given train of thought.

Thinking, if we now define it as a sequence of ideas, is of two kinds: associative thinking, and purposive thinking, or reasoning. In the former kind the idea of one thing calls up that of another by the associations of nearness and likeness; as when the thought of a sunset brings to mind a lookout from which we once saw it, or a prairie fire. The ideas in a drifting train of mere associations are of relatively concrete wholes. In the latter kind we are under a controlling interest which marks the partial aspects of things, and so orders our ideas of their properties and relations as to bring about a systematic understanding of the world. Reasoning, that is, involves analysis and synthesis. The concrete detail which our senses give fused together in things, it disengages by a selective interest for which certain details only are pertinent. These details or aspects have by dint of repeated comparisons between things taken on a general or *conceptual* character: they

[1] G. F. Stout: *Manual of Psychology*, Bk. iv., p. 466.

are factors common to many objects and processes. But the interest that guides this analysis is intent on articulating its disengaged concepts into new and significant wholes. A free synthesis results, for which the somewhat sketchy character of ideas is an actual advantage. The full detail of an object of sense is irrelevant to the ideal whole in which it becomes an object of knowledge. Knowledge calls for a new kind of determinateness. What is vague in the several ideas is made definite by their mutual relations within the ideal whole.[1] The primary thing of crude experience gives way to a conceptual thing of far more worth for the intelligence. The former shows its qualities and relations only "in the lump" and as immediately given; the latter shows them as elements of a larger system of things.

Reasoning makes constant use of language,

[1] G. F. Stout: *op. cit.*, p. 467. It would be more accurate to say that what is general in the ideas is thus made specific, for the vagueness in an idea-image does not give the generality to its meaning. A sketchy mental image of a house can more readily refer to the general notion 'house' than can one full of particular detail. But logical generality lies in quite another sphere from perceptual vagueness, and within that sphere it is precise, "being a matter not of momentary existence but of intent." When the image is not a picture of the meaning but a symbol, it is more fit if particular, as when the notion 'house' is thought of by means of the specific word-image *house*. "Words, distinct in their own category and perfectly recognisable, perform very well the function of embodying a universal: for they can be identified in turn with many particulars and yet remain throughout particular themselves" (G. Santayana: *Reason in Art*, p. 74).

which affords names for its ideas, and signs for its ordering activity. The analysis required in reasoning is indeed a requirement also of speech, for the ideal wholes of thought are too composite and varied to be representable by single sound-complexes. Language, therefore, not only expresses reasoning, but helps it. The necessary serial occurrence of speech-symbols breaks up the object of thought into its partial aspects, and articulates these as distinct concepts or general ideas. For example, the sight of a man running brings to one's mind no distinction between the agent and his act; but as soon as one says, *the man runs*, agent and act appear as two elements of a sense-complex. *Man* and *run* here name concepts, while *the* and the *-s* of *runs* express the fact that these general concepts blend in the particular experience of the moment.

If each element of our thought were represented in speech by a wholly different sign, a vocabulary would be too burdensome to remember. Hence our speech-symbols must conform to some system, in which likenesses of sense find a correspondence in likenesses of sound. On its formal side, therefore, language is a system of uttered sounds (a limited set for any one language), which may be varied by arrangement, stress, pitch, tempo, and pauses, and which with their written signs are economically organised as a medium for conceptual thinking. On its mental side it presents ideas with their relations and the speaker's or writer's attitude toward them. On either side its complex wholes can be analysed into comparatively stable units—ideas, letter-sounds—capable of many combinations; but as one unit is added to another, each resulting combination becomes a formula narrowing down to a single application. The speaker starts with this complex meaning, passing it on item by item to the hearer, who thus starts with the uttered formula. Language therefore serves rather to plot out the points of contact between mind and mind—their knowable identities, than to clothe any total consciousness. The whole flux of mental life, indeed, is infinitely subtle and electric, and sentences are at best but partial conductors for its discharge.

Language is thus a mental-mechanical complex which offers matter for studies other than grammar. Since words and sentences are units of thought, one cannot describe them in more than an external way without having recourse to the mental sciences, psychology and logic. Psychology deals with speech on both its sides: (1) with the reflex and unwitting processes of utterance by which words take shape; (2) with the train of thought which they express. It may either describe what now goes on in the speaker's mind, or it may explain present words and idioms by what has gone before in the collective speech-forming mind. Thus one may look simply to one's own associations with *serpent, snake,* to compare the image and emotional value now attaching to each; but etymology shows that the early idea of 'serpent' took the name from the impression of its 'creeping.' Words, however, so far as they can be treated apart from sentences (in which alone they have their actual being) belong to semantics and the dictionary. Psychology bears upon grammar when it treats of the complex ideal wholes behind word-groups: for example, when it ascertains whether in thinking them one proceeds from words to sentences, or from sentences to words.

Logic shows its common ground with grammar in such terms as 'subject,' 'predication,' 'substance,' 'attribute,' 'abstract,' 'hypothetical.' Since formal logic deals only with sentences of assertion, grammar has undeniably suffered from efforts to describe the manifold facts of speech in terms reflecting an artificially limited view of the facts of thinking. Modern logic, however, gives more heed to varieties of mental play, and has much to offer in explaining the kinds of judgment and the grammatical categories of 'noun,' 'verb,' 'mood,' etc.

By tradition grammar is divided into accidence, describing the forms of words, and syntax, explaining their uses, in sentence-structure. Practically this is convenient, but by thus introducing flectional forms in paradigms, that is, as they attach to notional units, our text-books confuse at the outset their grammatical point of view with a lexical one. The fact that OE. *stānes, stāne, stānas, stāna, stānum* occur as forms of *stān* is purely the affair of the dictionary. Grammar has to do with the uses of these forms: it must resolve into syntax. The two fields, it is true, cannot be kept wholly apart. Flectional forms commonly serve at once to show a word's sentence-relations and to carry some element of its independent meaning, as that of number, tense, degree. Many words, as *paenitet, ought, must,* have uses peculiar to themselves. And particles, such as *shall, of, but, than,* can hardly be defined at all except in terms of their function in discourse.

Since grammar and dictionary together make the basis of rhetoric, it is evident that their account of speech must be critically sound as far as it goes, before the latter can attempt any valid theory of style.

Grammar and Practice. Grammar differs from any natural science, such as botany, in that its subject-matter is a means to an end. The forms and combinations of words are conditioned at every step by expressive purpose, so that one has not only to describe them but to judge of their fitness. Where confusions of word-form defeat the ends of expression it is just as right to call them "ungrammatical" as it would be absurd to call a hybrid plant-form "unbotanical."

As a medium of expression language is conditioned on "usage"—the consensus, that is, for employing the same forms and formulas in the same senses. But in society as we find it this consensus is never perfect. Geographical and social differences within it are bound to give dialectic and illiterate speech, and since differences of this kind are marked off from what is standard not by sharp lines but by a penumbra of doubtful forms, it seems legitimate to expect that grammar should make clear some norm of practice. Men's habits of speaking, aft[illegible] all, are in some measure under their control, and if for any reason a disputed usage can be decided for the better, they have as much right to make a choice here as in other matters of conduct. An interest in grammatical practice has in fact been exercised in modern times from two points of view.

The older point of view looked towards the ideal of a perfected language. To ascertain, purify, and fix usage was the aim of the Accademia della Crusca and the Académie française, an aim that influenced the English wits under Queen Anne and the Georges,[1] and is still apparent in old-fashioned grammars that emphasise what locutions are to be held "correct." The failure of this ideal has followed from two defects. In the

[1] It gave Dr. Johnson the selective principle for his dictionary. See P. W. Long: *English Dictionaries before Webster* (Papers, Bibliograph. Soc. of America, vol. iv., 1910).

first place it assumed that language could be rendered stationary, whereas a living speech is constantly and inevitably undergoing changes. This does not mean that radical changes in it take place suddenly, but that in doing service for millions of speakers and for many generations a language becomes modified by the different habits of utterance and thought which it encounters. Thus speech-sounds vary slightly in passing from father to son; words expand or narrow in meaning; some forms grow obsolete while new ones appear; and locutions are continually affected by the tendency to ellipse and by the influence of analogy. In the second place the older grammarians conceived their standard too rigidly. Usage for them was either "correct" or "incorrect," and they took little account of the expressive gain in having a choice not only of sense but of flavour—literary, colloquial, rustic, etc. Their opinions, therefore, seem committed to a bias for maintaining in speech a sort of feudal caste of things absolutely proper and absolutely improper,—an unscientific attitude sure to betray one into persecuting free expressions that cut across the grammatical "rules."[1]

[1] A lesser mischief here consists in *interpreting* idioms in a fashion that admits of being described by the regular categories. I have seen a pedagogical paper aiming to show that *but* should always be "parsed" as a conjunction. Thus, *he is but a child* = *he is, but* (he is) *a child!*

The point of view now uppermost looks especially to understanding speech as a development. It values any fact, whether from classic writing, dialect, or slang, that gives evidence of the processes that make language a living and growing thing. Its interest, indeed, is purely scientific, taking the facts as they are, without venturing theories as to what they ought to be. Philologists of to-day, therefore, are averse to any conformities in language that do not seem spontaneous. Its evolution, they feel, should not be "personally conducted." Their concern with practice takes the form of pleas for colloquialisms that a bookish standard would exclude. Indeed the reaction from pedantry now amounts almost to a Rousseauist partisanship for the slip-shod as something especially natural and "alive." Expressions such as *if I was you, the man who I saw, let everyone do what they like*, are called "spoken" English, where teachers of the old school would say "illiterate"; and the tendency to discard the subjunctive is mentioned without comment as to any loss or gain involved.[1]

[1] "It [the subjunctive] is practically extinct as a living form, surviving only in a few isolated constructions" (H. Sweet: *New English Grammar*, vol. ii., p. 108).

G. P. Krapp (*Modern English*, New York, 1909) puts the *laissez faire* attitude toward usage explicitly. Thus the discriminating use of *shall* and *will*, *lie* and *lay*, *like* and *as*, etc., he views as merely "academic," the concern of "theoretical grammar."

As against dogmatism and the tyranny of artificial rules, such a liberal tone is salutary; but it easily misses certain discriminations that sound science as well as sound practice must call for. It is apt to give the uninformed an exaggerated idea of the changeableness of speech,[1] and to foster a notion that sense-association and phonetic law are what *determine* usage. Of course they *influence* usage, but their working is wholly subject to men's need of conveying to one another distinctions of meaning. Language at bottom is simply a social utility, and the fact of its evolution does not debar an ideal of its progressive betterment. Some betterment one can always promote by adopting speech-forms that add distinctions, either by specialising a locution already in use that has merely duplicated another, as in *I do fear it; he is come*, which once meant nothing more than *I fear it; he has come;* or by taking up a locution newly offered. Now while in the main stock of a language words and grammatical forms do not lie in any one plane of discourse, they divide elsewhere into different levels: vulgar, colloquial, bookish, poetic. A speech-form, that is, may have *connotation*,[2] a flavour taken from its habitual

[1] See, for example, Baskerville and Sewell: *English Grammar*, p. 11, where it is intimated that the changes of twenty years may be expected to put *any* grammatical statement out of date.

[2] Since "connotation" in the logical sense has other names,—*intension*, *implication* (see p. 94),—the term seems more useful in this rhetorical sense.

context, and making part of its expressive value. Hence its use in every proposed instance must take account of fitness not only in its meaning but in its associations. Where the older grammarians failed was in overlooking the fact that dialect, colloquialism, and even slang may in given cases meet an expressive purpose. "*Them that was n't bald was beardless*" in Henley's poem carries an effect that would be spoiled by *those that were not*, etc. But the enthusiast for "live English" makes the opposite mistake of talking as if any scruple between formal and familiar uses were pedantic. If he means simply that the familiar must not be stamped "incorrect" *for all contexts*, no one can demur; but one may grant that *it 's me* suits well enough a context of unbuttoned ease, without wishing to retranslate Matt. xiv., 27: "*It 's me; be not afraid!*"

Since these connotative "levels" do not make any sharp cleavage from one another, we shall find expressions that savour uncertainly. Disputes as to fit usage, therefore, give us two sorts of cases to deal with:

(1) Cases in which connotation is not in question, either because it is unmistakable, as in '*it 's up to you*'; or because it is neutral, as in '*to wholly agree*.' Such cases are disputable only on the score of meaning, and should be adjudged by their actual usefulness. Appeal to literary authority is here irrelevant. A writer can always

disown slanginess in a phrase by quotation marks, if it fills a real expressive gap; and if "splitting" an infinitive (*tiresome to always go tiptoeing about; enough to quite prove a faulty use*) makes a distinction that he needs, it is nothing to him that Dryden and Jeremy Taylor did not need it.

(2) Cases where connotation is in doubt. An expression may have its connotation changing. If it otherwise fills a need, a speaker will naturally wish the benefit of the doubt as to its associations. Here an appeal to authorities is of course legitimate. In making it, however, one must guard against certain fallacies by which it is commonly vitiated:—One must bear in mind that a noted speaker or writer is not necessarily a student of language, so that if authors add authority, it is by their practice, not by their opinions.[1] Moreover, one does not show an author's use of a phrase by citing the mere fact of its occurrence. One must cite the whole context, and also his use of alternative phrases. Pleaders for a disputed form are always offering a list of famous names to justify it, as if its *existence* in reputable speech were in question. What one wants to learn is *how* it occurs: whether, that is, the cited authors use it

[1] Anyone who cares for the ungracious task can easily collect a fund of untenable opinions on usage from great writers. Thus from Coleridge: "A language which, like the English, is almost without cases, is indeed in its very genius unfitted for compounds" (*Biographia Literaria*, p. 2, Dent, 1906).

colloquially or seriously, in casual slips or in habitual practice.

It is evident that our text-books describe "good use—national, present, and reputable" in terms that impose too passive an attitude upon the pupil. He who disregards an archaic or slang connotation in a speech-form will of course strike a false note with it. Otherwise, if it makes for precision, he need not ask "authority" to use it, nor wait to see what the language is going to do about it, for his own practice is part of what the language is "doing."

II. THE SENTENCE-RUDIMENT

Judgment and Concept. The primary act of thought, by which the mind wakes up to the meaning of what is before it, is Judgment. Thus I judge, when, seeing a white object in the landscape, I observe that it is a church. My sense-perception brings it as an indeterminate part of reality before my mind, which then judges by referring to it the meaning for which language has the name or fixed symbol, *church*. By sensation, as James says, I become aware of it; in judging, I begin to know about it.

A little scrutiny of this account of judgment will disclose that it simply describes in different terms what we have already shown purposive thinking to consist in: viz., a development of ideal wholes by analysis and synthesis of ideas. To see something as 'a white object in the landscape' is to begin with an idea[1] of it: to observe that it is a church is, on the one hand, to "disengage by a selective interest" one of its aspects—viz., its use—

[1] The content of an idea may of course be any matter-for-thought: a sensation, thing, property, relation—whether, as here supposed, actually perceived or only remembered or imagined—or even such a purely formal notion as 'difference,' 'inversion.'

that has significance as a general idea; on the other, to recognise this idea as uniting with the given one in the ideal whole, 'white-object-seen-is-a-church,' which has thereby gained definiteness as something *understood*. The process is not so much one of combining two notional elements previously separate—something thought of, plus something thought about it—as one of disclosing an element previously latent in a single notional complex.

After calling judgment "the primary act of thought," we may seem to go back on our words in thus showing it to involve ideas or concepts, which therefore appear to be items of thought that it presupposes. Formal logic, indeed, has expressly taken them as such, and given the process by which one attains a concept a special name—"simple apprehension"[1]—to distinguish it from judgment. A closer view of what concepts are will clear the matter up. In the first chapter we called the notional content of thinking, ideas. Now the significant fact about ideas is that they develop. Beginning in the child as hazy notions imperfectly applied, they gain determinateness as the life of reason advances. The idea 'gold,' for example, is at first merely that of something 'yellow,' 'smooth,' 'hard,' 'used for coin and personal ornament.' To this notional complex experience adds further items,—'costly,' 'malleable,' etc.,—until one arrives at the scien-

[1] E. g., Jevons: *Lessons in Logic*, pp. 11, 12.

tific concept 'gold,' bringing all these particulars and others—'metallic element,' 'specific gravity 19.27,' etc.,—within a definition at once full and exact. But to notice that something is yellow, malleable, costly, etc., is already to make judgments about it. One's thought has asserted a defining relation between the vague sketchy thing-notion with which one began and certain recognised attribute-notions. Again, to have even these simpler ideas, 'yellow,' 'costly,' means that one has passed judgments identifying a colour, a set of value-relationships. That is, to have an idea at all is to have the result of one or more judgments. Once had, an idea takes on the general character of a concept by dint of successive judgments which disclose its sense-elements as factors common to other ideas. A concept, therefore, is simply an idea at some stage of its progressive definition by judgment. As an item of knowledge it no more exists apart from the medium of judgment than does its symbol, a word, exist in speech apart from the sentence. It is essentially a comparatively stable judgment-aggregate, recognised and named as a starting-point for further judgments. Hence, to say that judgment involves concepts merely amounts to this, that every act of judging starts with the thinker's present state of knowledge. Whether a state of knowledge be described in terms of judgments or of concepts will then come to the same thing: for, on the one hand, each concept sums within itself the same sense-relations that judgments overtly articulate; on the other, each fresh judgment is simply the recognising in analytic terms of a development in conception.

The Proposition. The unit of speech that gives explicit form to a descriptive judgment is called in logic a Proposition. It is the simple assertory sentence. Since symbols of speech must occur in a series, the two ideal elements of a judgment: (1) the more or less undefined matter given; (2) the defining idea, appear in the proposition as distinct members, the Subject and the Predicate. By thus seeming to begin with a subject and to add a predicate the proposition disguises the real transition in its thought, which is not from *S* to *P*, but from *sp* to *SP*. One does not begin with two ideas—'that white object' and 'house'—lying apart in the mind, and then judge by superposing the latter. The interest impelling one's judgment brings the object under view from the first as something to be described by its use,—indeed with its use-aspects so stressed as almost to show an adumbration of 'house' within it. Judging simply draws this whole complex into sharper focus where it yields the propositional form: *that white thing is a house.*

The subject-term need not always be as explicitly expressed as the predicate. For example, when someone entering the room exclaims, "*Hot!*" we have a proposition in which the subject is simply accepted as a present sense-impression, while the predicate is the explicit term *hot* defining it. Many exclamatory words such as *Good! Shame!* which are traditionally classed as Interjections, are really predicates of this rudimentary type of proposition, and would be better called sentence-words (pp. 91–2). Certain other propositions of this type are called Impersonal, since their subjects, in each case the given content of perception, are not specified by distinct ideas. Such are: *It rains; methinks; him list; es macht heiss; mir traümt's; me paenitet; pugnātur.*[1] The subject may be designated without being named; as in, *This is hot; here goes!* But in fully developed propositions both subject and predicate are named as explicit concepts. Thus: *I am hot; Babylon fell; the floods came; rex vicit.*

Psychologically, the simple assertory sentence expresses the articulation of a conceptual whole into such of its elements as are pertinent to the interest guiding the train of thought. This interest reinforces associations that determine not only what conceptual whole shall at any moment be thus analysed, but what factors shall thereby result. The notional complex behind *Babylon fell*

[1] Impersonals are not the most primitive form of judgment: (1) They are more numerous in later speech, (2) ancient grammarians understood subjects with them: ὁ Ζεῦς ὕει, etc.

contains many elements which the speaker disregards in making the particular analysis that yields this sentence. Under a different interest it will yield other conceptual elements: say, *Babylonians gave over their city to Cyrus*. The process of finding words for a sentence is therefore primarily that of bringing to light within a somewhat dimly defined thought-composite its at once defining and relevant concepts. When this conceptual segmentation is once clear, the words follow almost of themselves.

The limits of a proposition are thus imposed by its relation to the train of thought as a whole. The latter passes through one conceptual complex after another, lighting up within each, like motes in a moving ray, those elements which further its leadings. Within each, accordingly, two stages mark the analytic process off: (1) that in which the fresh complex is brought under view; (2) that in which it takes on determinateness. These two stages so dominate in one's consciousness of the process that they draw the issuing series of concepts into two groups, which appear in the sentence-structure as subject and predicate. Distinctness of subject and predicate, in fact, make the speech-complex a proposition, even if its elements are not words, but parts of one word. For example, *amāvī* unites three conceptual elements, 'love-did-I,' which show both terms of a proposition. Whenever in the history of such a sentence-word slurring and contraction in its sounds obscure the marks of these terms, it is because a fresh ordering of speech-material has brought them otherwise into view. Thus *amāvī*, 'love-did-I,' has given place to *j'ai aimé* (*ego habeō amātum*), 'I did love.'

The Copula. Since the proposition takes the form of two members related as subject and predicate, it may have a distinct particle of speech to express *the fact of their being so related.* This particle is the Copula. In its own character it expresses simply the fact that something is affirmed or denied, so that strictly speaking *is* and *is not* are the only true copulas. These two forms are said in deductive logic to determine the "quality" of a proposition, that is, its character as affirmative or negative—for the defining of an idea by a proposition can of course take place negatively, by what it excludes. In the artificial view of judgment that logic assumes (see p. 102), the copula appears as a distinct member in the proposition. Grammar, however, takes it as part of the predicate, which is thereby understood to express: (1) the idea predicated; (2) the fact of its predication. A pure copula, expressing the second of these two items and nothing else, hardly occurs in the languages we usually study. Instead of such we find either copula-words that carry in addition some element of the idea predicated (as *fuit* and *was* express its past occurrence); or words for the idea predicated that imply the copula (as *speak, amat,* and all "finite verbs").[1]

The two-part structure of a proposition allows it to be viewed as essentially the developing or defining of a subject idea by a related idea in the predicate. Two relations, therefore, obtain at the same time between these terms: (1) the relation which judgment develops between their meanings; (2) the subject-predicate relation which asserts that the former relation holds. The nature of the former may be indicated by a special particle; as in, *His dwelling is i n the mount; judgment is o f the Lord; senatus Hannibal-is erat:* but when its nature is sufficiently evident from the meaning of the terms, it need not be further expressed, and may then *seem* to be carried by a copula-word.[2]

[1] The meaning of the copula is of course present in every proposition, because it is essential to judgment. Since every judgment makes its assertion *ultimately* of the thinker's world as a whole, having for its immediate subject a selective perception or idea which is continuous with his system of reality (Bosanquet: *Logic*, vol. i., pp. 78, 83), its assertion must always be thinkable as true. From carrying this reference to reality, the various typical copula-forms show another use in which they are no longer simply copula, but affirm actual existence. For example: *Whatever i s is right; And Enoch w a s n o t, for God took him.*

[2] This apparent variety of meaning in *is* and *is not* is taken for fact by K. O. Erdmann: *Die Bedeutung des Wortes*, (Leipzig, 1910), p. 42: " Die Kopula spielt eine mehrfache logische Rolle und drückt ganz verschiedene Beziehungen aus."

For example:—

Snow is white (Substance and attribute).

Whales are mammals (Species and genus).

Two and two are four (Equivalence).

A square is an equilateral rectangle (Identity).

Tout comprendre est tout pardonner (Cause and effect).

The fact that the *meaning* of words here counts in the grammatical expression of their relations, shows at the very outset of sentence-study that the formulas of syntax cannot be viewed as if they had nothing to do with the separate word-meanings treated in the dictionary. Both word-units and word-group formulas are less precise in themselves for the fact that they exist only for each other, and always get a mutual delimiting in actual discourse.[1]

The Subjective Element in Discourse. Thus far our account of the sentence-rudiment has not made enough of the speaker's concern that it presupposes. We have remarked that a purposive interest determines how far its sense-complex takes analysis. But it is precisely this *relevance* of its meaning—the satisfying of an active interest —that gives a sentence the dynamic value that distinguishes it from inert matter-for-thought. Logically, *the wine is red* shows nothing more than

[1] E. P. Morris: *Principles and Methods in Latin Syntax*, pp. 46, 47.

the red wine; but psychologically it shows a live reference to truth, a relation that is quite external to *the red wine.* Both expressions carry an identical relation between *red* and *wine* as a fact of their meaning; but the former stresses it further as something *to be acted on*, as what can be reckoned one of the facts of life. On its mental side, therefore, the sentence represents a meaning plus a kind of emphasis that projects it into the field of vital concerns. This latter, subjective, value is quite overlooked in schoolbook definitions of the sentence as "the expression of a complete thought." Grammar has here followed formal logic in looking solely to the *content* of ideas as they lie before one, whereas it is their *direction*—a relation that lies, so to speak, in another dimension—that gives the peculiar sentence-completeness, a completeness like that of a closed electric circuit.

The nature of the speaker's concern offers a ground for classifying sentences even in their rudimentary phase. A sentence that issues from the impulse to extend knowledge takes the form of assertion. Here the subjective element shows merely as a dogmatic quality, not thought of as specially expressed. That the speaker views his assertion as fact is taken for granted. But the same sentence-content (e.g., *you are good*) may be projected non-committally (*if you be good*), or as question (*are you good?*), as command (*be good!*), etc. Here there is still *something* asserted: viz., the nature of the speaker's concern, for these formulas may be so cast as to show this feature objectively, as in, *that you be good is my wish;* but whatever assertion they carry is incidental to their purpose to be acted upon in a particular way.

This qualifying of the utterance by the speaker's attitude toward it may be expressed either by special words or by some change in its given sentence-elements,[1] such as grammar discusses under "mood." Examples of the former are *possibly, doubtless, perhaps, hardly; forsan, ut opinor;* of the latter, τεθναίης, *utinam moriāris, vous puissiez réussir; nun wären wir ja fertig damit.*

The speaker's feeling that gives the distinctive value expressed by a sentence-formula should not be confused with other emotional elements in speech. The feeling shown in a querulous tone or a drawl need not make any part of the speaker's expressive intention. Even though it is interpreted by his hearer, it seems outside of the linguistic convention between them, and is felt as something adventitious. Many words, again, have an emotional value as an integral part of their meaning. Thus *eventide* means *evening* plus

[1] H. Oertel: *Lectures on the Study of Language*, p. 287. M. Bréal (*Semantics*, ch. xxv.) here includes the "ethical dative" as conveying the speaker's interest in what he says: *he plucked me ope his doublet and offered them his throat to cut.* Even in the second person it is perhaps still felt as such: *a' would manage you his piece thus; il vous prend sa cognée.*

a sense of its poetic associations; *doggy* means *dog* plus an implied endearment. This connotation is an element of the word when taken by itself; and as such it falls outside the province of grammar. But the speaker's feeling conveyed in *patria floreat; his fall, happily, broke no bones*, attaches to the meaning, not of any one word, but of the whole sentence. Its expression, indeed, may be attached to a single word, but that is merely one of the mechanical economies of speech. In any case it is understood as something carried by the sentence as a whole.

III. THE WORD

Word and Sentence. It is now clear that in speaking a sentence we begin with its thought as a complex whole, which we then unravel into the ideas that issue word by word. To define a sentence, therefore, as a "combination of words," is to describe this process from the wrong end.[1] If we began with discrete ideas, matching the words for them together like dominos, we could never launch into an involved sentence as we do, without heeding where they were going to bring us out. These verbal idea-units, indeed, show but an artificial separateness as they lie on the page. Actual utterance makes in *let all acclaim the king!* no division by pauses. About the only pauses in utterance are those giving "breath-groups," which answer in part to sentences.[2] Of the separate words we are hardly conscious in talking, and even in writing the ancients did not divide them. The sentence, then, is the prior thing; the word is something analysed out of it.

[1] E. P. Morris: *op. cit.*, p. 45. The view of a sentence as something arrived at by combining words is common in text-books; e. g., Nesfield: *English Grammar Past and Present*, §1.

[2] H. Sweet: *Primer of Phonetics*, p. 42.

Within the sentence words mark off from one another what are felt as sense-items stable enough to take a like form in other sentences. Now an item of thought gets its independent identity by recurring in different contexts, much as things in the outer world become identified as such by recurring in different surroundings. If there were nothing in the nature of ideas to make them differ in the ease with which they can be thought apart, we should expect each idea that recurs to take a distinct word. But a difference in the separability of its parts is the striking trait in our stream of thought. This difference has been described by James as giving the contrast between what he calls its *substantive* and its *transitive* elements. The former are our concepts of things, qualities, happenings, "whose peculiarity is that they can be held before the mind for an indefinite time"; the latter are the observed relations that obtain between substantive elements. Of these two elements the former so dominate by their greater stability in consciousness, that the categories of 'thing,' 'quality,' 'happening,' give the bulk of word-forms in every language. Transitive elements, on the other hand, are hard to see for what they are in themselves. What experience gives us is always things in relations. Only by an effort of abstraction can we think of relations apart from things; and the effort is apt to defeat itself. "As a snowflake caught in the hand is no longer a snowflake but a drop, so, instead of catching the felt relation moving to its term," we catch the substantive term, in which the relation is statically taken with its intrinsic quality quite evaporated.[1] Ideas of relation, therefore, are apt to be less independently expressed than substantive ideas. In a given language and period their rendering reflects the analytic habit of some one people, so that in general it varies all the way from mere formal marks attaching to words for what is *in* relation, to distinct words. If we call the notional content of the whole sentence a group-concept, we shall recognise in its words the series of concepts at which its analysis comes to an end.[2] The analysis may arrive either at distinct words both for the concepts and for expressing the fact and manner of their relations, or at less ultimate words expressing the concepts with more or less of their relational fringe. As sense-units, therefore, the words of one language show no such coincidence with words of another as is shown between their sentences. A Greek sentence and its English equivalent, though in each case variable as to form, have in common a fixed logical unity. But the corresponding Greek and English words, though alike in having their forms somewhat fixed, carry different implications as to the context in which they belong.

[1] W. James: *Principles of Psychology*, vol. i., p. 244.
[2] E. P. Morris: *op. cit.*, p. 45.

Any sound or sound-complex is a word, if it is used independently as the fixed symbol of a meaning. Thus in *the marble portals did unfold*, the sound-complexes thus separated in writing are words, since each keeps an identical meaning in any of numberless combinations. But *un-* of *unfold* and *-s* of *portals*, though they have meanings, depend for keeping them on being joined respectively to the beginning and end of other sense-units, and hence are not classed as words. Certain words, however, are only relatively independent. The "articles," for example,—*a*, *the*, *le*, etc.,—and the *to* in *to have*, *to see*, etc., are logically parts of other words which they must precede. "*To* see is *to* believe" is the same as "see*ing* is believ*ing*." But they are freer than *un-* and *-ing*, in that they admit other words between themselves and the words they belong with; as, '*a* fair *hit;*' '*le* grand *homme;*' '*to* clearly *see.*'

The thought conveyed by a sentence we have noted to be a complex, presenting three aspects: (1) ideas; (2) their relations as judgment-elements; (3) the speaker's attitude toward what he expresses; i.e., his feeling as to its reality, desirability, etc. For "substantive" ideas, and for any other ideas thought about, a language will have names: as, *horse, blue, chastise, quiescence.* If now it uses distinct words to express each of the other two aspects—their relations and the speaker's feeling—it will make propositions representable by the formula:

$$N—r—(f)——N'$$

Paris is doubtless grand.

where N,N' = names; r = relating-word; f = feeling-word, which in the example occurs parenthetically within the proposition. The same word, however, may express more than one aspect; thus:

$$N——rf——N'$$

Fashion may change;

where *may* both marks the predication of *change*, and expresses the speaker's feeling that the proposition states not fact but possibility. In fact, words that name ideas are apt to be modified or given some distinctive expression so as to convey at the same time either their relation, or the speaker's feeling, or both. Propositions, therefore, very commonly take the form:

$$N^{r}——N'^{rf}$$

Patria floreat!

The fatherland (may it) *flourish!*

in which *patria* is marked as subject-word by the ending *-a; floreat*, as predicate by the ending *-at*, which also expresses wish on the part of the speaker. If we admit as features of a word its position and tone of utterance, we must regard all name-words as possible sense-complexes of this kind, and represent any such proposition as "*Time goes!*" by the formula $N^{rf}—N'^{rf}$; since *Time* is here marked as subject-word by its position; *goes*, as predicate by the ending *-es;* and the speaker's feeling, by the exclamatory tone of both words. Apart from the sentence, therefore, we cannot define the whole possible meaning of the word, since it derives a variable implication from its setting. And since this varying element of sense may either give varying forms of the word (*dominus*, *dominī*, *dominārī*), or may be otherwise expressed for the same form (*man rules*, *a man milliner*, *they man the boat*) we must admit that the word as sense-unit is not a thing of fixed identity.

Kernel and Formative. Since words are complexes both in sound and sense, language economises in its demands on memory by using the same speech-elements in different words for identical elements of meaning. If a language always used sounds so diverse as *slave* and *servile*, *death* and *kill*, *a good play* and *well played*, to denote senses that have so much in common, learning its vocabulary would be as hard as learning to write Chinese, and for the same reason. But the more general distinctions expressed in these word-pairs may be so made as to retain in each resulting word an identical part to represent a sense-element that they share. Thus the notions of character, manner, state, causation, expressed in *servile*, *well*, *death*, *kill*, may all be expressed for *slave;* as, *slavish*, *slavishly*, *slavery*, *enslave*. In most words, therefore, one may distinguish ultimate sense-units of two kinds: (1) a nucleus (e.g., *slav-*) representing the dominant idea; (2) an added element or elements (e.g., *-ish*, *-ly*, *-en*) representing a sense-category or sentence-relationship in which this idea appears. The nucleus of a word, which is comparatively independent and often occurs as a word by itself, may be conveniently called its *kernel.* Thus, "Every inch a *king;*" "His state is *king*ly;" "Thy *king*dom come!" Added elements (*-ly*, *-dom*, *ge*mach*t*), which depend for their sense on being joined to the kernel, are called *formatives.*

This distinction between kernel and formative, made by the linguistic feeling of the speaker, must not be confused with the etymologist's distinction between stem and affix. A Roman of Trajan's time felt *serv-* as expressing the essential notion 'slave' common to *servus*, *servī*, etc.; and *-us*, *-ī*, etc., as determining the particular aspect in which that notion entered into discourse. To him, therefore, *serv-* would be the kernel of those words; *-us*, *-ī*, etc., formatives. He would probably not know that instead of *servus*, *servī*, his early forebears said *servos*, *servoi*, in which they felt *servo-* as kernel, and *-s*, *-i* as formatives. But this latter fact is what gives the modern student of Latin his ground for distinguishing *servo-* as the historic stem of a set of forms (with *-s*, *-i*, etc., as affixes), which he classifies as "cases" of the same word. Both distinctions, of course, are somewhat artificial ones, made for the purpose of describing a group of words taken as related—in the former case logically; in the latter, etymologically.[1] Kernel and stem, formative and affix, very often coincide; as in *princep-s*, *dis-passion-ate:* so that we shall probably create no confusion by calling formatives, as well as affixes, prefixes, when added before the kernel; as, *en*slave, *un*well, *ge*macht, *ἔ-λυον*; and suffixes, when added after the kernel; as slav*ish*, king*ly*, flow*s*, gemach*t*, *ἔλυ-ον*.

Naming and Relating Features in Words. Both kernel and formative word-elements and simple words that are ultimate sense-units like them, show a further distinction arising from the part they play in the sentence. The sentence-rudiment has already been remarked to contain: (1) judgment-elements; (2) some sign of their relationship as such. Word-elements and words serving primarily as symbols of ideas thought about, —ideas of things, qualities, acts, states, relations, appearing (at least when broadly considered) as subjects and predicates—are on this ground called

[1] The term "kernel" was suggested by Professor Jespersen, who illustrates it by *ēag-* in Old English *ēage*, 'eye,' as distinct from the historic stem *ēagan*. "If OE. *ēage* is said to be an *n*-stem, what is meant is this, that at some former period the kernel of the word ended in *-n;*" while, as far as Old English itself is concerned, it means simply "that the word is inflected in a certain manner."—*Progress in Language*, p. 144.

Naming, Presentive or Notional, elements, and Names: as, *king, sweet, loud, em-balm, strik-ing, wave-let, heathen-ism.* Word-elements and words serving primarily as signs that certain judgment-relations obtain between given ideas are called Relating elements and words: as, *of, to, since, if, and, shall,* write-*s*, *in* corpor-*e* san-*o*. It is necessary to define naming and relating features respectively as *primarily* symbols of ideas and *primarily* signs of sentence-relations, because while word-kernels may always be viewed by themselves as names, affixes and particles (that is, formatives, or simple affix-like words) are usually both naming and relating in their force, and one of these two features merely predominates. Thus *slave* is clearly a simple name; but *en-* in *enslave* not only, like *the* in *the slave*, stands for an element of meaning, but makes *enslave* forefelt as a predicate term.

Notional affixes and particles usually bring an idea in the word or phrase which they form under some general category of thought. Thus the formatives in *un-well, child-hood, mak-er, care-less, re-instate*, mean respectively the negation, state, agent, privation, and repetition of what the rest of the word means; and the particles in *a* man, *the* man, *some* man, *any* man, mean that an individual is taken respectively as simply one of a class, as a particular one, as one not yet specified, and as chosen at random. Notional formatives are what we call "derivative" prefixes and suffixes as distinguished from flectional ones.

Relating particles are peculiar in their meaning. James calls them "signs of direction in thought," and remarks that such combinations of them as "*either one or the other*, . . . *although it is so, yet*—are verbal skeletons of logical relation, blank schemes of the movement and adjustment of ideas."[1] This would reduce them to mere signs of the mind's ordering activity, which in fact some grammarians would make them, saying that they "have no meaning by themselves." The true account of relating particles, however, is made by Bosanquet,[2] who notes: (1) that they indeed have meanings: thus, *at*, *to*, mean relations which have the names *presence*, *direction*. But (2) that instead of naming relations as ideas thought about, they express the fact of relationship between ideas. Their meaning presupposes terms to be related, and is not complete without them. We can say, *They are of the world and f o r the world;* but we cannot say *Of is not f o r* in the sense that *R e d is not g r e e n.* Hence while such particles may mean certain relations of space, time, cause, etc., their special character lies in their indicating that

[1] W. James: *op. cit.*, vol. i., p. 252. On an earlier page (245) James does justice to the individual meaning of these forms: "We ought to say a feeling of *and*, a feeling of *if*, a feeling of *but*, and a feeling of *by*, quite as readily as we say a feeling of *blue* or of *cold*."

[2] *Logic*, vol. i., Introd., p. 20 f.

the words or word-groups they belong with stand in certain sentence-relations. That is, they qualify the meaning of the sentence primarily by setting out its form.

A language which expresses sentence-relations chiefly by relating formatives has its words grammatically classed by these into the groups called "declensions" and "conjugations." In each group a set of formatives with any given kernel make up what are regarded as the "inflected forms" of one word, shown arranged as a "paradigm." It is important to remember that such formatives are often notional as well as relating. Thus the flectional forms *box*, *box-es; engulf-s*, *engulf-ed; domin-us*, *domin-a*, show in each pair a distinction of sense. In *domin-us* the part taken by the formative may be shown thus:—

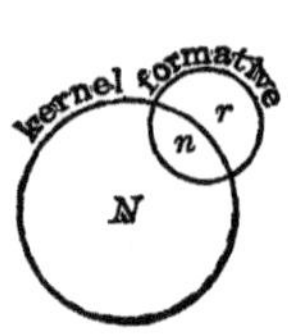

in which *r* stands for the distinction of subject-relation, and *n* for that of male sex. A highly inflected language, such as Latin, may have formatives with enough sense-elements, naming and relating, to turn the word into a sentence. Thus in *amā-rem* (*I should love*) the formative expresses: (1) predication; (2) the person of the speaker; (3) the speaker's attitude toward what is said; (4) a distinction of time. Such a fusion of meanings in the formative is called Polysynthesis.[1]

[1] H. Oertel: *op. cit.*, p. 289.

The naming and relating aspects of a word are sometimes called respectively its Content and its Function. Its content, then, is the dissociated idea which it presents when taken alone; its function consists either in bearing, or (in the case of a particle) in marking, a sentence-relation. Thus in *Presence at court was required*, the content of *Presence* is the idea of a certain space-relation; its function is as subject to *was required.* The particle *at* has a content almost identical with that of *Presence;* but it has the function of constituting *at court* a qualifying term in a certain sentence-relation to *Presence.*[1] The general sense-category expressed for a word by a notional formative or by sound-change has sometimes been distinguished as its *modal* content from its kernel notion or *material* content.[2] Thus in *drive, drove; ox, oxen,* words of like material content have in the categories of tense and number different modal content.

[1] The distinction of *content* and function as here made does not seem open to two objections which might be offered to that of *meaning* and function as discussed by E. P. Morris (*Principles and Methods in Syntax*, pp. 199–202). To distinguish function from "meaning" suggests that to represent sentence-relation is not just as much to have meaning as to represent any other element of sense; and to include in "function" the distinction of agent, means, result, etc., is to confuse these relations, which are distinguished by the content of words, with sentence-relations, which (as the next chapter will show) are constituted as such only by the structure of the sentence as a system of judgment-elements.

[2] Strong, Logeman, and Wheeler: *Introduction to the Study of the History of Language*, p. 74 ff.

An interesting process in word-history occurs when the function of a naming word in course of time grows so important as to make its content secondary. Thus *shall* originally meant 'owe' (cf. German *schuldig*, 'indebted'), but from its use in the sense of 'is bound to' 'is to,' as in *he shall go*, its content in *I shall go* has faded into the mere futurity of the act which its function is to predicate.

The Grammatical Classification of Words. Since words are the smallest *stable* sense-units in language, it is natural that grammatical study should have produced a scheme for classifying words in sentence-analysis. By their functions words would seem to be readily divisible into: (1) sentence-words; as, *mehercule, yes, good!* (2) particles, which either, like *the true, any man, to be kind, per aspera, ex nihilo*, can only contribute their element of content or function to phrasal terms of syntax, or, like *and, as, sed, vel*, are connectives; (3) words which can of themselves serve as terms of syntax. Even this division, however, while it follows their most general differences of use, draws no sharp line between the words themselves. Thus, *mehercule* is simply a clipped form of *mē Herculēs (juvet)*; *good!* is not a different word in *good for you!* and *certainly* may occur either as an emphatic *yes*, or as an adverbial term. Particles, also, are not felt as different words when, as in, *that may be, have you any?* they become terms of syntax. At the very outset, therefore, it is evident that to classify a given *use* of a word is not to make the word out as a distinct identity for that use. The identity of a word is both grammatical and lexical: that is, it is a matter not only of function but of content and form. This becomes clear as we pass on to subdivide the third and main class just given: that of words serving themselves as subject, predicate, attributive, and adverbial terms.

To begin with an example from analytic speech (see p. 67), the Chinese *ta*[4] (大) is to Chinese linguistic feeling the same word, whether used as *great*, *greatly*, *greaten*, or *greatness*. Here an identical form, referring (as do its English equivalents) either directly or indirectly to a like meaning, keeps through various functions a felt identity as a name. In such cases the name is the word. The function, shown by word-order, etc., is viewed as something relative and non-essential arising from its uses.

In inflected speech the name does not thus show as a distinct entity, since the naming kernel always appears with a formative, which gives the whole word-form a more complex meaning. The formative, in effect, carries for the word a little fringe of context that limits its function, and that may affect its content, either, as we have seen (p. 40), by adding a sense-element, or by causing a shift from direct to indirect naming such as occurs between *this is John* and *this is John's*. In the forms *bellum*, *bellī*, *bellō*, what gives identity as of a single word is the fact that *bell-* names their common content-notion 'war,' which, however, they express only in the sense-complexes 'war—as subject or object' (*bellum*), 'relation-to-war—as attributive (*bellī*) or adverbial (*bellō*).' The same kernel names another idea,—'wage war,'—for another set of forms, *bellāre*, *bellat*, *bellāvī*, etc., expressing other complexes of content and function. *Bellic-*, again, gives still another idea, that of 'derived from, or pertaining to, war,' for *bellicus*, *bellica*, *bellicum*, etc. Three sets of forms here constitute three "words," in each case by virtue of (1) a felt identity in content, like that given by the predominant partial in a complex musical tone; (2) a somewhat fixed rôle as regards function. Inflected speech, therefore, gives us only the "forms of a word." The word itself is an abstraction.

If now we would classify words, we must settle what changes of content, function, and form give variant forms and uses of one word, what give distinct words. But such a triple ground of classification leads into a tangle of cross-divisions. Content and function do not determine forms precisely. The same variation of form may mark, in one class of words, a difference of sense; in another, a limiting of use. In *bonus servus*, *bona serva*, the formatives *-us*, *-a* distinguish sex for the kernel *serv-*, while they merely restrict function for the kernel *bon-*. So in *this foot, these feet*, the "mutation" expresses for *these* not a plural content, but use with a word of plural content. Within the same language a given sense-complex is expressed, now by two words (*rubēre coepit*); now by a modification of one (*rubēscit*); sometimes by alternative constructions of the same word (*id tempus* or *id temporis*, *dator divitiārum* or *dator divitiās*), sometimes by alternative forms belonging to different words (*bellī gloria, bellica gloria*). Even if such alternatives are not actually identical in sense, an effort to classify their members by sense alone would involve one in over-subtleties. The distinction of "parts of speech," which consequently appeals now to meaning, now to form, cannot be carried out consistently. It must be evident that a sense-unit whose sense may be anything from the mere indicated function of *to* in *to see* to such a complex of meanings as *amārem* is too variable to serve as a valid unit for grammatical analysis. Since a conceptual complex has no actual existence apart from contexts which variously colour and qualify it, there is no assaying it into elements or aggregates of elements so fixed and precise as to impose units for words to match. Meaning alone, that is, does not offer the limits which should mark off a word. It is not a difference in either kind or amount of meaning that makes *amā-bam* one word, and *amātus ēram* two. Nor does a separability of its parts offer a sure *formal* distinction of words in a sound-complex. In speaking, one often utters a whole word-group as the unit, without being conscious of any separate items within it. Thus *Quae cum ita sint* may be felt and said simply as 'wherefore;' *in regard to*, as 'concerning;' and in such phrases as *so to speak*, *ut ita dicam*, *for that matter*, *qu'est-ce que c'est*, the words make their appearance as such only when written out. A word-group of this kind sometimes remains stereotyped in use until one or more of its words lose the meaning with which it originally entered the group. The meaning of the whole can then no longer be made out from the present meaning of its parts, and the word-group becomes an idiom. Words in a group, again, may by shift of accent or other phonetic change lose their separate identity, so that the group becomes more or less completely fused into a single word: thus, (*to*) *break' fast'* has become (*to*) *breakfast* (brĕk'-fȧst); *crudelī mente*, *cruellement*. In many cases such coupled words continue indefinitely as an "agglutinative" compound, within which they are felt as distinct constituent ideas; as, *servingman*, *inkstand*, *makeweight*, *porte-flambeau*, *Baukunst*. The word, in short, is a thing of somewhat uncertain and arbitrary identity; and conventional grammar, beginning with words as the ultimate "parts of speech," misses the true grammatical unit, which can be only some verbal equivalent of the judgment.

IV. THE SENTENCE AS ANALYSED

The Grouping of Concepts. Without attempting as yet a formal definition of the sentence, we can call it the expression in a word or words of the purposive articulation of a conceptual whole into such of its elements as further a given train of thought. Two aspects of the elements issuing thereby must then appear in its resulting verbal structure: their relations to one another, and a certain value for knowledge (as assertion, supposal, command, etc.) which they take as a sense-composite from the attitude of the speaker.[1] That the analysis expressed by a sentence follows a selective interest, points to the fact that the sentence is itself an element analysed out of a larger conceptual whole. The train of thought that takes form in a speech or essay does not come into

[1] Cf. Wundt (*Völkerpsychologie*, ii., 245): "Hiernach können wir den Satz . . . definieren als den sprachlichen Ausdruck für die willkürliche Gliederung einer Gesamtvorstellung in ihre in logische Beziehungen zueinander gesetzten Bestandteile." I have aimed to qualify and complete Wundt's definition (1) by taking account of the predicate relation, which I believe is always (at least implicitly) present; (2) by indicating how far the articulation is carried. Analysis of an ideal complex can always run to many elements, but in any given sentence it ends at factors determined by a particular guiding interest.

being point by point as its sentence-units appear. Rather is it something rising in the mind as a whole, and continuing behind its parts while these pass in turn through the focus of attention. We must therefore conceive our thought as a sort of notional continuum, which may undergo two or three stages of analysis before it begins to precipitate in words.[1] The whole content of a discourse thus begins as a conceptual nucleus, which will divide and subdivide by successive analytic impulses until it yields the elements that satisfy its speaker's expressive purpose. At each step the concept-group is felt as related to what precedes, and as stressing associations that determine what shall follow. Speech, of course, can begin at any point. "A whole oration might in an imperfect way be expressed in a single sentence: 'Catiline is dangerous;' 'Archias deserves citizenship.'" But if the words are hurried forward before an analytic step is complete, the sentence will be confused and stumbling. Once complete, "the fitting of sufficiently accurate words to the grouped concepts is almost automatic. Because thinking is so generally associated with words, the analysis is instinctively directed toward concepts which have before been associated with words. These are the natural ends towards which the

[1] E. P. Morris: *Principles and Methods in Latin Syntax*, (Scribners, 1902), p. 38. Chapter ii. of this work is a clear and interesting statement of the mental process here involved.

analysis moves, and when it reaches this point the words are already suggested. The only thing necessary, therefore, during utterance is that the concepts, grouped by their relations, should pass before the mind, or, more precisely, that the attention should be directed upon them in the succession which their grouping suggests."[1]

Sentences, therefore, should as sense-units be viewed in relation to the paragraph out of which they resolve. Within that unit of the notional continuum each sentence in its turn, while carrying over certain elements from what precedes, strikes up certain new ones, so that the whole moves off in successive complexes like a cadence-group of chords. The sentences get coherence from the concepts that, like "binding-tones," they sustain within the group; unity they get individually by stressing new concepts that are *relevant.* How this works out may be followed in a paragraph from Burke:

"*First, the people of the colonies are descendants of Englishmen. England, Sir, is a nation which still I hope respects, and formerly adored, her freedom. The colonists emigrated from you when this part of your character was most predominant; and they took this bias and direction the moment they parted from your hands. They are therefore not only devoted to liberty, but to liberty according to English ideas, and on English principles.*"

[1] E. P. Morris: *op. cit.*, pp. 41, 42.

If, disregarding variations of wording that give the thought here its nice adjustments, we set out the words through which it mainly leads, we shall have a series of five sentence-groups, in which the essentially new concepts may be numbered. We can then show the conceptual development of this paragraph by a diagram, making its notional elements begin their latent phase in the nucleus as dotted lines, emerge in the sentence as lines, and persist (like defining overtones) as broken lines. *S* and *P* mark subject and predicate; heavy lines mark the dominating ideas:—

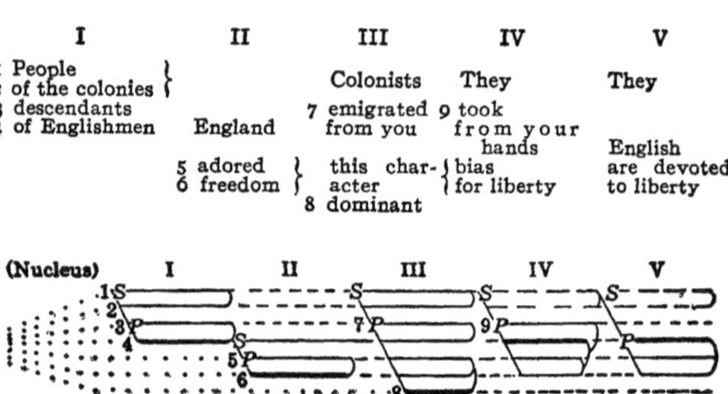

One will here remark first—what commonly escapes notice—how much any sentence in orderly discourse is apt to carry over from what precedes. Sentence iv. of course, so continues iii. that the two are punctuated as a compound; but sentence iii. likewise takes up i.: "*Colonists—from you* [*Englishmen*]" repeats "*People of the colonies—*

Englishmen." Generally speaking, the thought in a paragraph undergoes in the first part its definition, and in the latter part an emphasis of its trend. Thus most of the new concepts appear in sentences i.–iii. above, while sentence v. merely sums up the whole by stressing its leading ideas.

The second matter of remark in our example is the fact that the concepts do not follow one another through its sentences like beads on a string, but take a grouping by pairs. As a series in time, to be sure, they file through the centre of consciousness, but they show mutual defining relations of which each term may span more than one of them. This fact becomes easily apparent where the same concept is expressed now by a word (as, *colonists*), and now by a phrase (as, *people of the colonies*) in which its elements are derived from two other concepts. If we designate our conceptual units above by their numbers, we shall find their disposal within the sentences about as follows:—

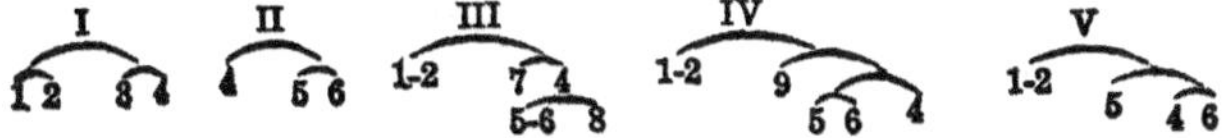

The first pairing here evidently parts the sentence into subject and predicate. It remains to see what causes the further pairing, and what relations hold between the further terms.

Concept-phrases. To think at all to any purpose has been shown (p. 5) to involve analysis.

Its aim is always to identify in their mutual relations the conceptual factors of what has come to mind as vague matter-for-thought. Hence even apart from any analytic requirement of speech—and thought without speech is quite possible—one's thinking would begin with an undefined notional composite, and end in definite concepts. The analysis in that case would end precisely at such concepts as disclosed the nature and trend of the whole, whether or not these were such as could be matched by words. But when thinking proceeds in terms of speech, its analysis must end in factors that are at once conceptual and verbal: and since language never has enough single words to match every thinkable sense-complex, it must constantly improvise in analytic terms expressions for which no single words exist. One has only to compare two versions of the same thought, to realise that the language-medium itself offers planes of conceptual cleavage that the analysis must reckon with. Take, for example, the following in Greek and in English:

Φιλοκαλοῦμέν τε γὰρ μετ 'εὐτελείας καὶ φιλοσοφοῦμεν ἄνευ μαλακίας.

"*For we are lovers of the beautiful, yet simple in our tastes, and we cultivate the mind without loss of manliness.*"[1]

Not only does the Greek sentence divide the

[1] Thucydides, ii., 40. The translation is Jowett's.

thought between fewer and less ultimate words than the English, but it sets out the resulting ideas in a different order and adjustment. The English, moreover, makes explicit certain ideas that are only indirectly (if at all) implied in the Greek: for example, the notion of agent in *lovers*, and the specific notions 'taste,' 'manliness.' Strictly, one cannot call the thought the same in both. Yet since the English aims to translate the Greek, one must conclude that its differences result from conflicting principles of structure, each medium tending to crystallise the thought into forms proper to itself. One can indeed imagine a speech-medium so fluid as to comply with every free articulation of disembodied thinking, but actual speech always more or less conditions what kind of articulation is possible. What is possible, again, often gives place to what is rhetorically preferred. *Φιλοκαλοῦμεν* above is used for *φιλοῦμεν τὸ καλόν*, evidently because it answers formally to *φιλοσοφοῦμεν*. The form may thus add to the thought an unforeseen beauty of musical effect.

A primary condition of the precise terms at which expression will arrive consists simply in the existence or lack of names for given concepts. Now the question as to *what is named* brings under view the fact that the world of our practical interests mirrors itself in the mind as made up of things and their qualities, behaviour, and relations.

Qualities, indeed, are prior in the mind to things, since we know any physical object—say, a piece of chalk—only as the spatially defined fusion of its sense-aspects—'white,' 'dry,' 'brittle,' 'adhering to what it rubs,' etc. Logic traverses this whole notional field with two categories, those of Substance and Attribute. Qualities, properties, behaviour, relations, are all attributes of things; and in everything that which has the attributes is conceived as substance. Both substance and attributes, as thought of apart from any actual concrete thing (as when one thinks of "brittleness" without thinking of chalk, glass, slate, or other brittle thing) are abstract ideas. Substance, moreover, is a mere conceptual fiction. It is our habit to conceive an orange as *something having* the attributes 'roundness,' 'yellowness,' 'fruity structure,' 'pliancy to squeezing,' 'fragrance,' etc. But could we strip from it, one by one, its being round, yellow, fruity, etc., nothing would remain over to be the orange. With these two categories we can begin mapping off the conceptual field into *kinds* of meaning, and since the kinds of things and complex attributes seem classifiable by the number of attributes defining them, one might think to arrange all concepts as generic and specific in series of ascending complexity; as, 'organism,' 'animal,' 'mammal,' 'hoofed quadruped,' 'horse;' 'Hellenic,' 'Attic,' 'Athenian.' One could not carry such a scheme far, however, without finding that changes of meaning get changes of name only when the latter are a felt need. Thus when qualified as 'young,' the concepts 'man,' 'horse,' 'pigeon' get new names, *child*, *colt*, *squab;* but 'sparrow,' 'eel,' 'toad,' do not. The named kinds of red—*pink*, *vermilion*, *scarlet*, *russet*, *crimson*, etc., if compared with a scale of red tints, shades, and hues, would fall at intervals almost haphazard. Language, that is, develops names for concepts that are practically important, without caring what unnamed gaps lie between them. Hence among different peoples one will find great differences in what is named. The Chinese, for example, having a special regard for blood-relationships, use two names each for 'brother,' 'sister,' to distinguish elder and younger in each case; and two each for 'grandfather,' 'uncle,' etc., to specify the relation as on the father's or mother's side. One might say that for speech all sense-complexes divide by their importance into 'stock' concepts, which take names, and 'nonce' concepts, which get only a roundabout expression.

Language may be said to meet the problem how to designate swarms of nonce-concepts with its comparatively small stock of names, by bringing them under the categories of generic and specific. Any thing or attribute can be viewed as of a certain *kind* by virtue of traits or aspects distinguishing it from its similars. Hence one can always conceive the notion of it—say, that of 'white horse'—as given by a mutual limiting of two other notions (as, 'horse,' 'white') each of which, though having an application too wide, yields a complementary quota of its meaning. Thus while we have no name for 'horse of white colour' (answering to *mare, filly* for 'female horse,' 'young female horse'), we can describe it by *white horse* as 'that sort of horse which is a case of whiteness.'[1] And while for some kinds of 'running' we have specific names (*trot, canter, gallop,* etc.), we can phrase expressions for many other kinds and instances by contraposing *run* with other generic attribute-names; as, *run quickly, run north, hares run by leaps.*

Since the two terms thus phrasing a name for a nonce-concept actually make a partial analysis of its meaning exactly as a sense-complex is analysed between the terms of a proposition, their inter-relation is identical with that between subject and predicate. Its expression—whether by an affix, as in *Cæsar-'s command, radiant-ly white, statua argente-a, furor anim-ī;* by a particle, as in, *snows of yesteryear, march towards Rome, adroit au jeu, vivre en roi;* or by mere position, as in *red wine, box kite, run fast*—involves a latent copula, which makes such concept-phrases simply propositional

[1] Not, of course, that we actually think it thus, but that its thinkableness in this wise is what makes *white horse* a valid expression for it.

names. If one asks: Wherein then do they differ from propositions—*the white horse*, for example, from *the horse is white?* we must answer that the difference is not logical but psychological. *The horse is white* gives its content the dynamic value as matter-of-concern which is always carried by a proposition. But the propositional name, carrying in itself no such active imputation, remains in the inert status of any name.

The paired names which typically form a concept-phrase are thus expressive of a latent judgment-relation. Concept-phrases, however, may overrun their paired structure by one or more associated names; as in, *a nervous, swarthy, young violinist; ran through meadows into the sea.* In some cases these added ideas seem to have been wakened in the speaker during his utterance of the phrase, and by associations in it leading away from what he set out to express. The phrase then loses its unity as a name, or at any rate breaks out from the unity of the sentence. But where these ideas all preserve the same logical relation to one term in the phrase, they fuse together as a composite answering term, and do not efface the essentially two-part structure of a propositional name. A whole series of epithets may thus crystallise at one conceptual kernel, as in—

Animula, vagula, blandula
Hospes comesque corporis,

Quae nunc abibis in loca?
Pallidula, rigida, nudula.

The Sentence and its Meaning. Since the verbal elements into which a sentence resolves, thus divide and subdivide throughout by judgment-relations, the whole takes on an organic aspect, with the judgment as its biological cell. Not only does its thought move on as a whole by an explicit predicate, but where the thought is complex subject and predicate will each involve a propositional form. This may be implicit, as in *still waters—run deep*, or it may be explicit but subordinate, as in *the soul that sinneth shall die.* Beginning with a bare name, a sense-complex can in propositional name and clause dilate progressively into predicative focus; as, *sinner*, *sinful man* or *man of sin*, *man who sins*. The sentence itself is really a composite 'nonce-concept,' and since the concepts at which its analysis ends are still simply agglomerates of presupposed judgments, the whole amounts to a little system of judgments formed into a unit of discourse. It is never word-elements that are added together to make sentences, but sentences that organise words to express their judgment-elements.

As analysed the sentence shows its content in an artificially static phase, very different from what passes through its speaker's mind. The thought, 'Cæsar crossed the Rubicon,' rises as an instantaneous whole,—a unit, not a series of units. It is not a thought of Cæsar plus a thought of what he did, but the thought of Cæsar-crossing-the-Rubicon as one of the facts of history. Thinking it, indeed, involves a deploying of its elements into time, just enough to show their logical relations and give play to the associations through which the purposive train must lead, but it is not completely *thought* until they are taken in as defining a whole. Before it is spoken, and after it is heard the sentence is notionally one; as set out in words it is like a motion-picture in arrest, breaking up into parts that do not restore its real unity when statically added together.[1] Subject and predicate, therefore, and all that grammar "parses," appear as such only in an immobilised row of snap-shots at the thought, not in the thought itself. The assertion that *the man runs*, taken in retrospect with its ideal elements suspended, allows them to be compared and classed in ways that reflect our practical bias. We then speak of *the man* as what is "talked about;" *runs* as what is "said." In actual thinking we do not begin with a man and pass to a running aspect, but once we put these ideas side by side, they appear as subject and attribute. 'The man,' we feel, must

[1] Cf. W. James: *Pluralistic Universe*, pp. 217 ff. and Appendix A, on the part that concepts play in the mental flux. In *L'Évolution créatrice*, p. 323 ff., H. Bergson treats the same theme: "le mécanisme cinématographique de la pensée conceptuelle."

be the primary notion, because it attaches itself to our interests at so many more points than a mere notion of running. Exactly the same retrospective interest is what gives in propositional names the grammatical distinction of modified and modifying terms. In *white horse* the notion is a unit, and its expression makes no less and no more of a horse's whiteness than of a white's 'horseness.' *Cæsar's command, soldier of fortune, gaudium certaminis, pranced spiritedly, struck home,* are each felt by speaker and hearer as single concepts. Of the words so paired, one does not qualify the other, but both divide between them the function of a name. The view of adjective and adverbial "modifiers" as terms distinct and subordinate is a fiction arising in afterthought, and should not be allowed to obscure the real unity expressed.

V. THE MEANS OF GRAMMATICAL EXPRESSION

Syntax and the Resources of Vocal Expression. Grammar takes in as subject-matter all features of words that express relations of syntax,—the ordering of ideas within the sentence. If, now, sentence-structure is something integrated out of judgments, the grammatical functions of words may be summed up as the bearing (or in the case of particles, the marking) of—

(1) Subject-predicate relations, whether explicit, or "conceptualised" into propositional names; and whether as single words or as word-groups.

(2) Certain associative relations—connection, contrast, subordination, etc.—between words or word-groups.

(3) The speaker's attitude towards what is said —which really resolves into a judgment-relation.

The subject-predicate relation gives four terms into which a typical sentence may be analysed: the "bare" subject and predicate that together form the kernel of its assertion, and the conceptualised predicates that serve as their attributive and adverbial "modifiers." Where language is systematic and frugal with its resources it will make a given notion expressible as each of these terms by varying some feature of the same notional form. In such cases the lexical and the grammatical aspects of a word seem fairly distinct. But our sentences are so habitually cast as asserting a *happening* about a *thing* of some *kind*, that words meaning things, happenings, qualities are often forefelt as having subject, predicate, or attributive function. Without any distinguishing grammatical feature they carry the function as their syntactic Habit. Thus *attend* presumably predicates its content, so that we need only three variations—*attendance, attendant, attendantly*—to put the same idea as respectively subject, attributive, and adverbial. Here, as again in *soft, softness, soften, softly,* the affixes are thought of as giving distinct, derivative words, even when they carry little more than this change of "habit," and except for historical reasons might be viewed as forms of the same word. But it is possible to have different syntactic habit expressed for the same idea by wholly different words. Thus *good deed, speedy return* express attributively the same ideas that appear adverbially in *did well, return soon.* Grammatical function here becomes a lexical ground, for a choice between these words is really conditioned by the polarity that draws them to different points in the sentence.

Of the MUSICAL PROPERTIES of speech-sounds

(1) timbre constitutes the differences between the letter sounds, vowel and consonant, and distinguishes function—at least indirectly, by changing one form to another for different constructions, as *sing, sung, song; equus, equōs.* (2) Force is the degree of loudness or softness of a sound. The comparative force of speech-sounds, or stress, may be conveniently indicated in three degrees: strong (marked″), medium (marked′), and weak (unmarked)—although rhythm and emphasis bring out many more gradations of force. It is common to distinguish between word-stress, which stamps a group of syllables as a unit of rhythm and sense; and sentence-stress, which marks a word for its special function within a word-group. Word-stress may distinguish function between simple words; as, *ac′cent, accent′;* or by making a specialised compound of what would otherwise be a phrase; as, *wait′ing maid″, wait″ing-maid.* Sentence-stress shifts function freely within the same group. Thus compare—

That′ is-my opin″ion,
with *That′-is my″ opin′ion.*
The-coat′ which-I-had-made″,
with *The-coat′ which-I had″ made″.*
He-failed″ complete′ly- to-understand″,
with *He-failed′-complete″ly to-understand″.*

(3) Intonation or variation of pitch takes place in speaking not by skips from one note to another as in singing, but by glides in which the intermediate

degrees are heard. It is in constant play for expressing the mood of the speaker; and since that mood may be a feeling or attitude toward what is said, intonation often conveys logical function, especially by suggesting the bearing of what is said upon what precedes or follows. Thus since a falling tone expresses certainty, completion, it normally marks the end of a declarative sentence; as, *you will succeed*↘; and of a command; as, *Go*↘ *ye.* The rising tone, expressing expectation, incompletion, often turns a statement into a question; as, *you will succeed*↗? In this case the intonation, by putting in question the actuality of what is said, makes the whole sentence call for a confirming sentence-word. A drop to lower pitch, with a quickening of utterance, often marks a transition from the main thought to a parenthetic comment upon it; as in, *General Armistead,* ↘*the account goes*↗, *cried out: 'Boys, give them the cold steel!'*

Since speech-sounds occur in a series, they admit of being distinguished by TIME-RELATIONS. (1) Quantity, the comparative duration of syllables, makes important differences between words, but rarely marks differences between their relations, as in *mēnsa, mēnsā; frūctus, frūctūs.* (2) A change of tempo, however,—of the actual rate of utterance —and especially (3) pauses regularly set off words that have grammatical function as a group. Thus, *A slight pause, such as is marked in print by a comma, may suggest that a clause is to be taken as a single term within a larger whole.* (4) Repetition of letter-sounds within words is sometimes a grammatical device; as in, λύειν, λέ-λυκα; *pendēre, pe-pendī.* Repetition of words may serve to connect terms of syntax; as, *He set the rivers within bounds,—the rivers which feed the sea.* Not only is the position of letter-sounds a determining feature in word-structure (cf. *tip, pit*), but (5) word-order is in some languages a fixed means for distinguishing function. Thus compare *John called James,* and *James called John;* Chinese, *wo*[3] *ta*[3] *t'a*[1] (I strike him), and *t'a*[1] *ta*[3] *wo*[3] (he strikes me); *he had made it,* and *he had it made.* In Greek, ὁ λευκὸς ἵππος means *the white horse,* whereas ὁ ἵππος λευκός means *the horse is white.* So in Chinese: *ta*[4] *jên*[2], 'great people;' *jên*[2] *ta*[4], 'the people are great.'[1]

Relating formatives and words are perhaps the most direct means of expressing function. Words of the notional classes *thing, quality, act* or *happening,* give in some languages inflectional classes by the sets of formatives characteristic of each. A difference of content, therefore, is assumed in the

[1] Wundt (*Völkerpsychologie,* ii., 2) reckons position as one of the formal features of words by calling it "*inner* word-form." Other writers imply as much by talking, for example, of a "positional dative," as in, *he gave them laws.* The formal classes which this distinction conserves are part of our grammatical tradition; but since they are not consistent logical classes, "inner" word-form seems a rather unprofitable subtlety. To see datives, adjectives, etc., in a Chinese sentence often means looking at it "through Latin spectacles."

distinction between declension, comparison, and conjugation. Even in point of form inflectional classes take in more than formatives alone would give them, since inflection may also be made, not only, as has been noted, by sound changes and by differences of quantity, but by treating different words as in an inflectional relation; as *sum, fuit; goes, went; I, me, we, us.* Certain derivative affixes that do little more than change a word's "habit" are practically inflections; thus *dark* and *darkness* differ less in content than in function in: *dark was the sky,* and *darkness overspread the sky.*

Inflections show the function of words in two ways: (1) They may indicate the *nature* of each word's sentence-relationship; as in: *Fabius urbem commeātū prīvāvit.* (2) They may by the formal agreement between words called Concord indicate simply the *fact* of their connection, leaving its nature to be gathered from their content; as in '*vīn-um sit apposit-um;*' '*tog-a candid-a;*' '*la bon-ne femme;*' '*des gut-en Vater-s Kind.*' A kind of concord occurs in the so-called "sequence of tenses," where, as in '*Quanta cōnscientiae vis esset, ostendit*' ('He showed how great *is* the power of conscience'), a tense is changed from the one logically called for to one that marks a grammatical relation between clauses.

Analytic and Inflected Speech. The most striking fact in the grammatical history of the

Indo-European tongues has been the shift in structure by which the cleavage between naming and relating elements now passes not so much *through* their words (as in *Beat | ī mund | ō cord | e*) as *between* them (*Bienheureux | sont ceux qui sont | nets | de | coeur*). They have developed, that is, from an inflected, towards an analytic, type. Instead of attaching the expression of relations, of time-distinctions, and of the speaker's attitude, to notional 'kernels' by means of inseparable affixes and sound changes (*cant-ās, cant-ārem; sing, sang, sung*), they now tend to express these elements singly by independent words. The Old English Chronicle, for example, says of William the Conqueror:

"Betwyx ōðrum þingum nis nā tō forgytanne,—
Among other things [it] is not to be forgotten—
þæt gōde frið þe hē macode on þisan lande, swā
the good peace that he made in this land, so
þæt ān man, þe himself āht wǣre, mihte
that a man, who was himself aught [of any account], might
faran ofer his rīce mid his bōsum full goldes,
go [fare] over his kingdom with his bosom full of gold,
ungederad."
without harm.

In this sentence one notes that the words *other, things, good, this, land, gold* all appear with inflections which are lost in its modern version: *goldes*, for example, being "analysed" into two words that can show independently the notion 'gold' and the relation 'of.' It therefore falls to students of grammar to settle: (1) how this change has come about; (2) whether such a change betters or mars a language as a medium of expression.

Until very recently both these questions had answers which were in general acceptance. How inflectional loss has come about is explained by orthodox philology as follows: Its cause has been the working of "phonetic change"—the slow unnoted change which inevitably takes place in the speech-sounds of a people.[1] Phonetic change, occurring most readily in the unstressed endings of words, must in time break down the distinctions between formatives. Thus by Chaucer's time the vowels of the older word-endings (*mōna, sunu, stānas, lufode*) had become generally "levelled" to a uniform *-e* (*mōne, sune, stones, luvede*), which in modern English is wholly dropped. As word-endings became indistinct and uncertain as a means of expressing function, the language is thought to have developed significant word-order and relating words to make good their loss, and thus to have passed into the analytic type of structure.

On the question whether a flectional or an analytic tongue has the more expressive efficiency, learned opinion has long been governed by literary

[1] Another recognised cause is the working of analogy, which undoubtedly tends to bring into uniformity different inflectional means for expressing the same distinction. Thus Old English *bōc*, 'book,' had the plural form *bēc*, which should now be *beek* just as *foot* has *feet*. But *book* has followed the analogy of the larger class of words which take *s*-plurals. Analogy, however, leads to the discarding not of inflections *in toto*, but only of inflectional duplicates.

tradition. The power and beauty of Greek literature and the prestige of Latin as the language of culture through the middle ages have naturally given these tongues the first place in scholarly esteem. Moreover, the orderly arrangement of declensions and conjugations, and the readiness with which words may be classified by their endings into distinct "parts of speech," give an inflectional grammar an aspect of system and logic. It is not surprising, therefore, that the old inflected languages are generally thought to be richer in grammatical resources, more elegant and precise in setting a complex thought in its due perspectives, than a modern one with few relating endings and detachable relating words. Professor Santayana, for example, thus compares classical and modern speech:

"This beauty given to the ancients by the syntax of their language, the moderns can only attain by the combination of their rhymes. It is a bad substitute perhaps, but better than the total absence of form, favoured by the atomic character of our words, and the flat juxtaposition of our clauses. The art which was capable of making a gem of every prose sentence,—the art which . . . made the phrases of Tacitus a series of cameos,—that art is inapplicable to our looser medium. . . . Our modern languages are not susceptible of great formal beauty."[1]

[1] G. Santayana: *The Sense of Beauty* (Scribners), pp. 173–4.

The views thus summarised as to the rise and the value of analytic speech-forms are now stoutly challenged.[1] Phonetic change, it is admitted, was the proximate cause of the "decay" of inflections; but no mere physical cause can be viewed as acting upon speech regardless of men's expressive intention in speaking. Before the analytic means of showing sentence-relations had developed, any tendency to slur relating endings would be constantly checked by the speaker's need of making himself understood. The change, therefore, more likely proceeded as follows: Fixed word-order began to appear within the inflected languages simply as a result of growing orderliness of thought. Relating particles were at the same time added to inflected words wherever the inflectional meaning was vague.[2] After word-order had acquired functional value, and the more precise relating-words were current, relating endings lost their importance, and would become assimilated, slurred, and dropped, from the natural tendency of speakers to trouble themselves over no more speech-material than is needed to convey their thought.

The expressive efficiency of inflections, again,

[1] See Otto Jespersen's *Progress in Language* (esp. pp. 96–111), a cogent criticism of the "down-hill" idea of the trend in language.

[2] Bréal (*Semantics*, p. 19) cites evidence that already in the Augustan age Latin had begun to make a free use of relating words. An inscription of 57 B.C. reads: '*Si pecunia **ad id templum*** (instead of *eī templō*) *data erit.*'

is over-rated. To begin with, their systematic and logical aspect is apt to prove superficial. Professor E. P. Morris says of Latin:

"The impression of system comes, no doubt, from the way in which we learn the facts of inflection. For the purposes of teaching, the grammars very properly emphasise as much as possible such measure of system as Latin inflection permits, producing at the beginning of one's acquaintance with Latin the impression of a series of graded forms and meanings covering most accurately and completely the whole range of expression. But it is obvious that this is a false impression, and so far as we retain it, we are building upon a wrong foundation. Neither the forms nor the meanings are systematic. . . . A glance at the facts of Latin morphology as they are presented in any full Latin grammar, or in Brugmann's *Grundriss*, or in Lindsay's *Latin Language*, where large masses of facts which defy classification are brought together, furnishes convincing evidence that irregularity and absence of system are not merely occasional, but are the fundamental characteristics of Latin form-building."[1]

The supposed precision of inflectional endings does not appear on any critical view of the whole range of their uses. Latin case-endings, for example, seem, as classified in the grammar, to make neatly definite constructions. But these con-

[1] *Principles and Methods in Syntax* (Scribners), pp. 52, 53.

structions owe their definiteness to the fact that the grammarian has taken account of stem-meanings and the context in classifying them. Without reckoning in the meaning of the stem one could not call "*gladiō occīsus* an instrumental ablative, *forō occīsus* a locative, and *nocte occīsus* an ablative of time. The variation in case-meaning even follows variation in the meaning of a single word. Thus *nomen consulis* would be a 'possessive genitive,' if *consul* designated a particular person, but it might be a 'genitive of apposition,' if *consul* stood for the office."[1] The genitive case in most of its uses—'partitive,' 'objective,' 'appositional,' etc.—can be described only by help of its context, that is, by reference to the combined meaning of its stem and of another word which it is taken with. In itself it is wholly vague. All the classical cases and moods have been minutely studied in the hope of fixing upon some original or primitive meaning (*Grundbegriff*) for each. But the results of this study add little definiteness to our notions of the flectional endings in themselves.

The richness of inflected words in relating marks would mean more, if many of them were not superfluous. What is gained, for example, by expressing for *ought* a distinction for the person and the number that 'ought,' as in *dēbeō, dēbent?*—or by repeating the formative for *I had* in *audīveram et spērāveram et pārueram,* 'I had heard and hoped,

[1] E. P. Morris: *op. cit.*, p. 71.

and obeyed'? In *duōrum bonōrum virōrum* the notional 'kernels' for *two good men* are actually unaccented, the stress falling only on endings which express three times over the relation 'of' and the plural number.

Where the same formative expresses two or more distinctions, it is not possible, as it is in analytic expression, to make one of them the point of remark by simple stress. Thus no shift of stress in *sperāveram* could make the distinction between *I had' hoped* and *I' had hoped*, while a mere shift of order, *had I hoped*, expresses a further distinction that in the Latin would call for added speech material. *Hominī* does not offer for separate notice the singular number and the function that appear in *to a man*, nor can it distinguish this sense from that of *to man*.

In arranging words, it is true, inflected speech admits of a freedom not possible when word-order makes distinctions of grammar: and free word-order varies rhythm and emphasis in ways which analytic speech can hardly imitate. Greek and Latin sentences must be conceded a surpassing degree of elasticity. In—

> *Quis multa gracilis te puer in rosa*
> *perfusis liquidis urget odoribus*
> *grato, Pyrrha, sub antro?*

the epithets are distributed where no English rendering can follow them; and no three English forms can express *deus mundum aedificāvit,* like the Latin, in six different arrangements. English, however, does arrange for emphasis, and (with the help of particles) quite easily: *the world was what God made; he who made the world was God.* If the Latin and English parallels do not produce identical shades of emphasis, it is because classical sentences move on a diminuendo principle, English on a crescendo, so that a like stress falls in the two types of structure at opposite points. Niceties of position have been the study of more than one modern who—

D'un mot mis en sa place enseigna le pouvoir,

and if Greek and Latin writers attain them more freely, they do so with offsetting disadvantages. Indeed they almost require the freedom so as to break up the iteration in their case-endings. The writer, perhaps, and not the language, should be blamed where periods, knit by many marks of concord, tend to evolve at rambling lengths; but it is significant that obscurities in the Greek masters commonly result from their efforts to win a telling conciseness with flectional polysyllables.[1] We may envy the Greek his "victoriously intri-

[1] W. Rhys Roberts: *Dionysius of Halicarnassus on Literary Composition*, Appendix A, p. 336. The introduction and notes to this text have valuable illustrations of classical and modern word-order, with a bibliography of the subject (p. 33).

cate sentence," contrived with "much adjustment to bring a highly qualified matter into compass at one view,"[1] but he would envy us the ease with which English turns off a forthright sentence at once unambiguous, elegant, and crisp.

If, therefore, putting aside the traditional prejudice, one compares the old and the modern tongues simply by the grammatical resources they offer, one must admit that the change from inflectional to analytic structure has made for economy and for closeness of verbal fit. Differences in sound-values, in idiom, and in the associations of words doubtless give to each language its special untranslatable qualities, but the same amount of speech-material will in our present languages do more expressive work.

Limits in the Change of Grammatical Forms. If in historical times the trend in our languages has been from a flectional towards an analytic structure, one may ask what we are to look for in them before and after this period. A review of their changes brings up at three questions: (1) From what sort of structure were the old flectional Sanskrit, Greek, and Latin derived? (2) Toward what structure do our modern analytic languages tend? (3) Does the nature of speech offer any *a priori* limits to economy and precision as the goal of grammatical development?

[1] W. Pater: *An Essay on Style* (Macmillan), p. 19.

Among philologists the theory has hitherto prevailed that inflected speech, in which formal elements are inseparable parts of words, is preceded by an "agglutinative" stage, in which these elements, while still occurring only as affixes to notional kernels, are felt as distinct sense-units, and can transfer their meaning by shifts of position. Such agglutinative complexes answer to the later flectional forms much as *cannot*, *manlike*, to *can't*, *manly*. Thus for Latin *ferimus*, in which the ending has no recognisable sense by itself, Sanskrit had *bharāmas(i)*, in which *-ma-si*, 'I-you' (i.e., 'we'), shows the identity of distinct old pronouns. The progressive fusion of such combined roots can be seen for comparative forms answering to *am*, *art*, *is*:—

SANSKRIT	OLD GREEK	LATIN	LITHUANIAN[1]	ENGLISH
as-mi	*ἐμ-μί*	[e]s-um	es-mi	a-m
as-i	*ἐσ-σί*	es	es-i	ar-t
as-ti	*ἐσ-τί*	es-t	es-ti	is

In such forms as *take*, *took*, and Arabic *qatala*, *qutila*, a formal distinction has penetrated the root itself.

Agglutinative speech, in turn, has been viewed as developed out of a primitive "isolating" stage, in which all the elements are independent and invariable root-words, expressing their sentence-relations exclusively by position, habit, and relat-

[1] Lithuanian (still spoken on the shores of the Baltic) is a remarkably archaic member of the Indo-European family.

ing particles. English, for example, would be an isolating language, if its sentences were always like *Saw they land? The ward boss will rue it! A ten-pound cod took the bait.* The typical isolating language is Chinese. Thus, for 'In different countries languages are different'—

Ko^{4}	*kuo*^{2}	*ti*	*yen*^{2}	*yü*^{3}	*pu*^{4}	*t'ung*^{2},
Each	land	's	speech	words	not	alike

the Chinese sentence makes a distinct word of the possessive sign, and implies a verb by its word-order. English also allows its possessive sign a word-like separableness (as in, *the boy we saw yesterday's father*), but this Chinese *ti*^{1} can pass into a relative pronoun; as in, *wo*^{3} *tso*^{2} *jih*^{4} *nien*^{4} *ti*^{1} *shu*^{1}, '(the) I-read-yesterday's book,' i.e., 'the book *which* I read,' etc. In *na*^{4} *kê*^{1} *liao*^{3} *pu*^{4} *liao*^{3}, 'that cannot be done,' *liao*^{3} is first notional verb (*done*), then auxiliary (*can*), and in *ch'ü*^{4} *liao*^{3}, 'went,' it is the sign of past tense. Chinese words, therefore, are one-syllable "roots," and Chinese sentence-formulas are chiefly a matter of their order.

If the numerous roots common to our languages (such as *sta* in Greek ἱστάναι, Latin *stāre*, German *stehen*, English *stand*) represent actual words in a primitive isolating tongue, within which declensions and conjugations arose by the gradual attachment of formal to notional words, we must view the rise of inflected speech as a transition from simple, clear, and economical formulas to complex and redundant ones. Thus for Latin we could not call it an expressive gain if the significant particles which once gave but one set of agglutinative forms for nouns, and one for verbs, had developed by phonetic changes into five declensions and four conjugations. And the whole analytic trend that followed in our languages must then have been actually towards an earlier type of grammar. There are strong reasons, however, for doubting that primitive speech was ever isolating. The roots that we can analyse out of words to which they are common express too preponderatingly ideas of action, to represent any complete language, and they express it too much in the abstract ('do,' 'make,' etc.) to reflect the very concrete thinking of primitive folk. Primitive tongues that we actually have among North American Indians, Eskimos, etc., show the very opposite of simple abstract units, lucidly arranged. Their utterances are long, repetitious conglomerates of concrete import, in which distinct units often can hardly be made out. Thus for 'bring us the boat' the Cherokee says, *nad-hol-i-nin*, a sentence-word that discloses general units, *naten*, 'bring,' and *amokhol*, 'boat,' only when compared with a number of like formulas containing them.[1]

[1] Cf. Eskimo: *aglekkigiartorasuarnipok*, 'he-hurries-away-and-exerts-himself-to-write,' and the examples cited from Santālī in the *Census of India* (1901), p. 280. E. B. Tylor's *Primitive*

Chinese, on the other hand, can no longer be assumed to be a primitive language. At least two facts point to its words having once been longer ones with formal elements: (1) "Tones" or musical glide-accents such as characterise Chinese words are found also in the Scandinavian languages, where their differences have been proved to answer to the contraction, in certain cases, of two syllables into one. (2) Word-order is the chief grammatical feature not only of Chinese, but of its kindred languages in Tibet, Burma, and Siam, which, however, have severally their own laws of word-position. No one of these sets of laws can be that of an isolating parent tongue, "for that would mean that the other races have changed it without the least reason and at a risk of terrible confusion. The only likely explanation is that these differences are the outcome of a former state of greater freedom."[1] But if the parent speech had no fixed word-order, it would

---

Culture (4th ed., 1903) has in chapters v. and vi. many illustrations from savage speech, bearing especially on its lexical beginnings.

[1] O. Jespersen: *Progress in Language*, p. 88. The *Census of India* (1901), p. 257, specifies some of these divergencies: "The Siamese–Chinese and the Mōn–Khmĕr families adopted the order of subject, verb, object, with the adjective preceding the noun qualified, while in the Tibeto–Burman family we have subject, object, verb, and the adjective usually following the noun. Again, in the Tai and Mōn–Khmĕr sub-families and in Nicobarese, the genitive follows the noun by which it is governed, while in Tibeto–Burman and Chinese it precedes."

have required something answering to formal affixes in order to express sentence-relations at all.

That the roots common to our languages originally had independent status as words it is quite unnecessary to assume. Rather is it more natural psychologically that just as sentences are prior in language to words, so words are to roots. In each case elements recurring in different sense-complexes drew to their expression identical elements in sound-complexes. Roots, therefore, are in most cases not older than the words we view as derived from them. They are simply etymologist's abstractions of what is common to a group of related words. When their identity as sense-elements has once been fixed in the *sprachgefühl* of a people, they may of course be brought into new formations, and there is no denying that some flectional forms of Greek and Latin result from the agglutination of roots previously more or less independent. But other flectional forms can be proved to have originated otherwise,[1] and there is no adequate ground whatever for believing that a general evolution has taken place from root-words, through agglutination to inflection. Such a belief assumes in primitive men a capacity for deliberate and laconic selection of the pertinent, for abstractness in sense-units and for a rational ordering of them, most unlike what is found among

[1] See O. Jespersen: *op. cit.*, pp. 67–71.

savages to-day. The Bantu languages in South Africa are voluble with iterative sounds that carry through their sentences a kind of profuse but irregular concord. From ten to sixteen inflectional classes for nouns give a riot of forms beside which the five Latin declensions seem simplicity itself. The evidence is strong, too, that these Bantu noun-classes have developed by a shortening of locutions that once gave still more numerous, redundant, and irregular formulas. What we should expect in the beginnings of speech is the slow adaptation of unmeaning chatter to the expression of concrete thought-wholes. Our proto-human ancestors must have had their vocal powers long before they did much at thinking, and their utterances would show much sound for little sense. This is still the case in truly primitive speech, with its "polysynthetic" sentence-words. Even in classical speech the approach to anything like rational system is still remote. When we find that Latin forms nouns of *action* with the suffixes *ā, io, iā, min, iōn, tiōn, lā, mā, nā, tā, tu, er, or, ōr,*[1] we can only say that it has for the purpose a mere welter of speech-material, as yet unwrought upon by reason. Now the strongest force at work in language is assimilation by analogy—a force that makes for regularity. In Latin "it is almost necessary to infer an earlier condition of less uniformity. . . . A syntactical method which

[1] G. M. Lane: *Latin Grammar*, §212.

presupposes an orderly development of meanings and forms from single starting-points is fundamentally wrong. . . . The movement has been all the other way, and the partial regularities of language in historical times are not the survivals of a primitive system, but indications of the partial victory of analogy and assimilation over the centrifugal forces in language."[1] For language as a whole Professor Jespersen sums up the trend as "a progressive tendency from inseparable, irregular conglomerations to freely and regularly combinable short elements."[2]

The view of inflected speech as traceable back through agglutination to isolating roots has led those who hold it to look for beginnings of agglutination and flection in the analytic speech of today. In Chinese, for example, it is not hard to find particles (like *mên*[1] in plurals *wo*[3] *mên*[1], 'we,' *ti*[4] *hsiung*[1] *mên*[1], 'brothers') that occur only as virtual affixes. French *donnerai* is a new flectional future from the analytical *donāre habeō* which replaced the old flectional *donābō;* and in spoken English *he 's, he 'll,* etc., can be called inflected forms. If such instances represent a pervasive trend, we shall have to think of our grammatical history as describing a sort of rotation,[3]

[1] E. P. Morris: *op. cit.*, pp. 55, 56, 62.

[2] *Op. cit.*, p. 127.

[3] G. v. d. Gabelentz (*Die Sprachwissenschaft*, p. 250 *ff.*) speaks of a "Spirallauf der Sprachgeschichte." See on this topic Wundt: *Völkerpsychologie*, vol. I., part ii., pp. 176–180.

from the inflected state to the analytic, and then through agglutination back to flection again. It must be doubted, however, whether any such general regression will come about. Fusion of speech-units can take place only in much-repeated formulas. At more primitive stages of thought the fewness of sense-modifying particles and the small formal range in their ordering might favour it, but in modern analytic speech fusion is opposed by their great number, and by the many significant variations of order which our more complex thinking calls for. It is hard to see how *he 's* can ever come to be felt as one word so long as in question and negation we say *is he? he never is.* In fact the possible means of expressing grammatical relations are always so manifold that one must guard against taking such terms as flectional, agglutinative, and isolating as applying to any language throughout. The differencing features they denote are often not characteristic enough to offer adequate ground for comparing languages even of different families.

Thus far the evolution of grammatical structure has been hardly if ever affected by any deliberate purpose among speakers to produce a system. Indeed, a proposal looking towards a concerted effort to shape usage is now apt to start an outcry against "schoolmastering the language." However, language is valuable chiefly as a social utility, and as civilisation advances it will probably not remain the only utility that is left to haphazard influences, with all its lacks and useless anomalies conserved by mere habit and prejudice. But any intelligent effort to improve speech must reckon with the fact that bare utility is not its only consideration. Speech is originally a sort of vocal music, and whatever in its expressive effects are pleasurable derive from qualities intrinsic in the medium. Euphony, assonance, rhythm, and subtle analogies between sound and sense impart harmonics of feeling-tone that permeate its representations. Literary quality, therefore, is possible only where its forms offer a choice. In point of bare utility there may be a waste in having two forms for the relation 'of,' two each for past and present tense, and two for comparative degree. But these grammatical superfluities can be turned to poetic account:—

The hounds of spring are on winter's traces.
Where joyous lovers kissed and clung.
Surge answers surge and deep doth call on deep.
More fine than moonbeams, whiter than the cloud.

A rigid economy that should use no more speech-material than is absolutely necessary to precise distinctions would reduce language to a vocal algebra. At least, utterance would become pithy and sententious rather than eloquent. It is significant that Chinese, which in the Northern Mandarin uses but 420 syllables (these being further distinguished by the four "tones"), has had little spontaneous poetry like the European folk-song,[1] though it is rich in popular proverbs. Language at its best, therefore, will find the due mean between music and a code of symbols. Rhetoric and utility are its centrifugal and centripetal forces,[2] which must work together to produce a structure lending itself at once to beauty and to the business of life.

[1] That in the *Shih Ching* or Song Classic of the Confucian canon dates, of course, from the early period when Chinese was probably not monosyllabic.

[2] G. Santayana: *Reason in Art*, p. 81.

VI. TERMS OF SYNTAX AND PARTS OF SPEECH

Words as "Parts of Speech." A modern, accustomed by print to think of words as units evident to the eye, feels surprise at the slowness with which Greek inquirers arrived at the distinction of "parts of speech" (τὰ μόρια τοῦ λόγου). By Theodectes and Aristotle these were reckoned as three: name-words, verbs, and connectives. Later philosophers, we are told,[1] made out successively the articles, "appellatives," pronouns, prepositions, and participles, and "divided the adverbs from the verbs." This last remark is interesting, for it suggests that verb-adverb phrases had been felt as the single "propositional names" we have described them to be (p. 56). The *Ars Grammatica* of Dionysius Thrax, our earliest school grammar (about B.C. 100), enumerates "noun, verb, participle, article, pronoun, preposition, adverb, conjunction,"[2] and proceeds to de-

[1] Dionysius of Halicarnassus: *De Compositione Verborum* (Roberts, 1910), ch. ii., pp. 71–73.

[2] Dionysii Thracis, *Ars Grammatica* (Uhlig), p. 23. The ancient views on grammar can be followed in Steinthal: *Geschichte der Sprachwissenschaft bei den Griechen und Römern* (2d ed., Berlin, 1890–91).

scribe them: the Noun as "a part of speech taking case-inflection, and meaning an object or affair, as *stone*, *schooling*, with an application either common, as *man*, *horse*, or proper, as *Socrates;*" the Verb as "without case-inflection but distinguishing times, person, and number, and meaning action either exerted or undergone;" the Participle, "sharing the traits of both verb and noun;" the Article (with which it includes the pronoun ὅς), "case-inflected, and set before or after case-forms of nouns;" the Pronoun, "a substitute-word for the noun, distinguishing person;" the Preposition, "a word used in composition before any other part of speech;" the Adverb, "uninflected, and qualifying the verb;" and the Conjunction, "setting the connection of thought in its order." The eight word-classes thus named were taken over by the Roman grammarians, who distinguished further the Adjective, which from its case-inflection had been reckoned a species of noun, and the Interjection, previously classed with the adverb.[1]

What these classes give is evidently a rather makeshift scheme of the word-forms found in Greek and Latin. Their prestige in grammatical tradition seems surprising when we note that they have little or no reference to the one grammatical criterion, that of function. In later times, it is true, much effort has been made to give them more logical definitions. Thus the common noun has

[1] H. Steinthal: *op. cit.*, ii., pp. 218, 219.

been said to name a thing directly, by association with all its essential attributes, whereas the adjective names it indirectly, as the bearer of a particular attribute, *white, true*, etc., while the attribute itself is named by the "abstract" noun, *whiteness, truth*.[1] Like definitions by content have been offered for verb and adverb.[2] But these can be carried out only by straining the facts of thinking. For example, the meaning of *snow is white* doubtless "comes to the same" as that 'snow is a white thing;' but it is not an identical thought. In language 3×4 does not equal $3 \times 2 \times 2$.[3] As the first grammarians, dealing with inflected speech, made their chief criterion form, so the modern, dealing with speech that is mainly analytic, tend to make it function, basing the noun on the subject-object relations, the verb on predication, etc. But our school grammars confuse their aim with the traditional one of classifying, not simply the

[1] Adolf Stöhr: *Algebra der Grammatik* (Leipzig, 1898), p. 1.

[2] For the verb Wundt (*Völkerpsychologie*, I., ii., 136) makes 'condition' or 'status' (Zustand), broadly defined, an essential content-notion; for Professor Sweet's definition of the adverb, see note, p. 145.

[3] Stöhr's account of the adjective fits only its "substantive" use, as in *the white and the blue; none but the brave deserve the fair.* It seems to reflect J. S. Mill's distinction between a "non-connotative" term, which means a subject only or an attribute only; as *John, whiteness;* and a "connotative" term, which "denotes a subject and implies an attribute;" as *man, white.* "The word *white* denotes all white things . . . and connotes the attribute whiteness" (*System of Logic*, bk. i., ch. ii., p. 15).

uses of words, but the words themselves, which, as we have seen, are constituted by meaning and form as well. Thus for nouns they drop the single appeal to function in *John's gospel; starvation wages; the troops were taken prisoner; I am friends with him; I'll devil-porter it no longer; slow and steady wins the race.* As a result we have a triple ground of classification which makes these categories of little scientific use, especially when applied to speech of an alien type. Chinese words, for example, lack the formal ground altogether. In the proverb—

> *Ch'u*^{1} *mên*^{2} *pu*^{4} *tai*^{4} *ch'ien*^{2}
> *Pu*^{4} *ju*^{2} *chia*^{1} *li*^{3} *hsien*^{2},
> 'Go(ing) abroad without tak(ing) cash
> (is) not up-to loaf(ing) at home,'

it is irrelevant whether we "parse" *ch'u*^{1}, *tai*^{4}, and *hsien*^{2} as verbs or nouns of action.[1] Even in English the parts of speech can be made out with assurance only in such "pattern" sentences as, *snow falls; snow is crystalline; white snow fell softly.* Since names of things have more *implication*, and names of attributes, wider *application*, most statements say what *things are* and *do*, and hence use typical nouns, adjectives, and verbs. But these labels often miss essential features of the thought, since even in a pattern sentence the

[1] In the Tibeto-Burman languages words of verb-function are inflected like nouns, and take subjects in the possessive: 'I go,' for example, is expressed *my going*.

stress (as in *John' comes to-day*) may distinguish a real predicate from the merely formal one. Live speech, in fact, keeps words in such unstable equilibrium that they develop transitions from one category into another. So long as grammar aims to pigeonhole them neatly into eight or nine classes, it must remain a mere "fair-weather" science, making a brave show of terminology where all is obvious, but collapsing as soon as exact discrimination begins.[1]

It is easier, however, to "muckrake" the parts of speech than to replace them with word-categories valid for every language. Sentences follow the same essential types in Greek, English, Chinese, and Polynesian, and show everywhere the distinction of notional and relating elements. But words in different tongues may combine answering features of content, function, and form, in such diverse ways that cross-divisions among them are inevitable. No scheme for "parsing" will escape confusion, that does not take one ground of distinction at a time, and classify the word not as something detached and absolute, but as it stands in a context. With these pre-

[1] Where conventional grammar does not break down itself, it tries to suppress idiom. Cf. Nesfield: *English Grammar Past and Present*, p. 89: "If for the sake of such ungainly phrases [he looked *quite the gentleman;* the play had *quite a run*] we are to say that adverbs qualify nouns, then what distinction between Adjective and Adverb would remain?" That is, we must not talk in ways that disturb our *a priori* definitions!

cautions we can through the present chapter make a shift with the old nomenclature. Thus, taking function as a ground, we have a broad but sound division between: (1) words used as terms of syntax; (2) particles; (3) sentence-words.[1] These classes we can then subdivide, taking in turn function, content, or form: thus—

I. WORDS SERVING AS TERMS OF SYNTAX. These subdivide by function as—
- i. Subject-words (nouns in their typical use), classifiable by content as—
  - (1) Common, (2) Proper, (3) Attribute, (4) Pronouns and numerals.
- ii. Predicating-words:
  - A. Notional verbs, showing distinctions of—
    - (1) Voice, Mood, Tense:—"modal content;"
    - (2) Number, Person:—for "concord."
  - B. Predicative nouns, adjectives, and pronouns.
- iii. "Modifiers":
  - (1) Adjective, forming "propositional names" for things.
  - (2) Adverb, forming "propositional names" for complex attributes.
  - (3) Substitute-forms for adjective and adverb (attributive nouns, oblique cases, and "case-phrases").

[1] H. Paul: *Prinzipien der Sprachgeschichte*, p. 353 (4th ed., Halle, 1909).

II. Particles, words that primarily mark sentence-relations—
 (1) Prepositions, forming "case-phrases" (phrases like *of man;* cf. *hominis*).
 (2) Auxiliaries, forming "verb-phrases" (*is white, may go*).
 (3) Conjunctions, forming "associative" word-groups.

III. Sentence-words, classifiable by content as—
 (1) Interjections.
 (2) Vocatives (names used "absolutely" in direct address).
 (3) Imperatives.

The first of these classes, that of words as terms of syntax, will be discussed in the remaining sections of this chapter. With them may be incidentally noticed the particles—except conjunctions, which fall within a section of the next chapter. Sentence-words, too, are involved later, in the distinction of kinds of sentence. The articles, except where (as sometimes in Greek) they serve as pronouns, are but movable prefixes, and not properly words at all. A number of the categories used above evidently call for more precise names. Cases of class II and III are so commonly unambiguous, that the old labels make little trouble, but those in class I should get names that are free from the lexical cross-associations carried by "noun," "adjective," "verb,"—terms which commit us to the effort to classify not the use, but the disengaged word.[1]

Subject and Noun. In its typical use the noun is subject-word in the sentence. Subject-function, indeed, is not made a criterion of a noun in school grammars (which, however, often bring it in by the back door in some such remark as that "the subject of a sentence always contains a noun or noun-equivalent") since a noun has also the regular construction as object. The object, however, though grammatically an adverbial term, is really a kind of obverse subject, and becomes the formal subject by a simple shift in the construction: *Luke wrote Acts; Acts was written by Luke.*

The division commonly made of nouns into "common," "proper," "collective," "abstract," and "material," since it relates to their content, would seem to be less the affair of grammar than

[1] My insistence on this point is not because, like Jack Cade in the play, I would have no men about that talk of a noun and a verb, for we need these terms for such cases above as are *formally* shown. But at present they betray school text-books that rest "parsing" upon function into tacitly retaining the other criteria. It seems wholly mischievous that pupils should be put on their mettle to use logically definitions that are not logically valid. What we need further are certain neutral terms, so that one could specify, for example, the "attributive" use of *cannon* in *a cannon foundry* without having to class it as either 'adjective' or 'noun' —terms that refer to its *average* context, not to the particular context under view.

of the dictionary. Since, however, it makes question of the use of particles and plural inflection affecting the structure of the sentence, it calls for some notice. A noun is not any more of a *name* for its content than are adjective, verb, and adverb for theirs; but whereas these latter habitually express their content predicatively through its *relations*, the noun as subject-word is felt as presenting its content absolutely, and hence has always seemed to be the name *par excellence*. Now every name has two aspects to its meaning: its Implication or content-notion taken as a disembodied concept; and its Application, the instances, actual or ideal, in which the content-notion is realised. Thus *a man* gives the content of *man* in its aspect of applying to a particular instance or embodiment. The total application of a noun is expressed by its plural: '*men*,' for example, make up the application answering to the implication of *man*.[1] These two aspects of names we shall find of account in any study of sentences that looks closely to what they *intend* to assert.

The notional classes of nouns rest on certain common-sense distinctions which give them a grouping about as follows:—

[1] By referring any concept to typical descriptive judgments—such, for example, as 'A horse is a hoofed mammal (is fleet, domesticated, etc.);' 'Rosinante (a barb, Clydesdale, stallion, etc.) is a horse'—one might say of its substance- or attribute-name *N* (e.g., *horse*) that the predicates of *N* make its implication, while the subjects of *N* make its application.

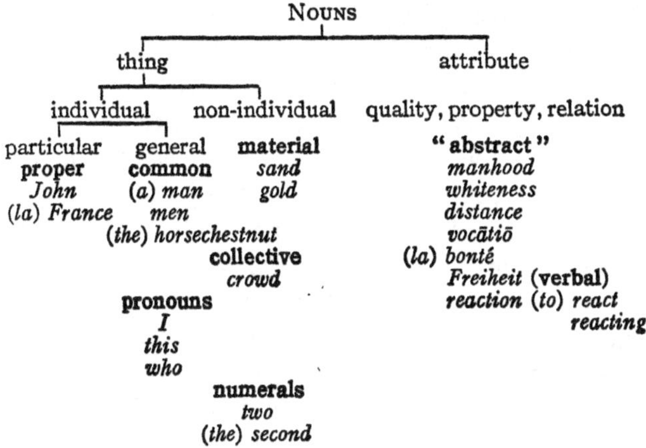

'Thing' and 'attribute' are categories which, though made much of in old-fashioned logic, we have remarked (p. 54) as offering a distinction that is convenient rather than real. A thing is simply a complex of attributes that has some independence in space and time; and any attribute, especially if complex, is felt as a thing, whenever we can experience it apart—as a colour, when it rubs off. For grammar this fact underlies certain considerations of word-form.

A thing is *individual* when it has inner proportions, such as are given to a watch by its mechanism, to a spoon by its shape, to a word by its accent, etc. Inorganic substances, and other things having only external proportions, are not thought of as made up of individuals, and seem not so much things as constituents of things. Thus we do not say *a clay* except as we mean a kind of clay. "Material" nouns are therefore felt as attribute-names: as Bosanquet remarks, "*gold* in *this is gold* is adjectival." This fact doubtless accounts for the decline in use of English adjectives formed with *-en* from material nouns;—*golden, silvern, oaken,* etc.—which are now generally archaic, the kernel being used both as noun and as adjective; as, *a gold spoon, a wheat* (formerly *wheaten*) *cake.* Individual thing-notions of general application give common nouns. These may be class names for such ultimate individuals as *man, tree, house,* or names for more complex individuals, as *nation, regiment, mob,* made up of units bound together by special relations. Between the two are collective nouns, as *crowd,* denoting aggregates of units bound together by the relation of number only. The same thing is often viewed at one time as a composite individual, at another as a mere aggregate; as in, *the jury consists of twelve men; the jury were divided.*[1]

A common noun differs from a proper one in having a descriptive value. It applies to concrete things by virtue of their having a certain set of attributes taken as distinctive of a *class:* that is, an imagined total of individuals, whether material and real or not, alike in these respects while differing in others. To define a common noun is

[1] Some grammars call *jury* in the first case the collective noun; in the second, a "noun of multitude."

to specify these attributes as a list of conditions to its application.[1] It is therefore a general name, not because it labels a genus—which takes an "abstract" name, as *mankind*—but because its application is conditioned. Proper nouns, on the other hand, simply designate individuals without special reference to their attributes. A proper name is fully descriptive only when, as in *a Daniel*, *a Crœsus*, some prominent attribute gives it a sense (as, 'wise man,' 'rich man') of wide application.[2]

Implication and application, or Intension and Extension as Bosanquet terms them, give the familiar categories of genus and species, general and particular, abstract and concrete, which underlie certain confusions in school grammar. A generic name, as *humanity*, labels the complex of attributes essential to a genus or class. *Man* in this sense is generic, whereas *every man*, *men* are general, applying to a total of individuals described thereby. A species is simply a sub-class,

[1] Alfred Sidgwick: *The Use of Words in Reasoning*, p. 249.

[2] The implication of proper names is a matter of dispute. At one extreme they have been considered as lacking it altogether, since the name given to a child, a town, etc., rarely has any reference to its traits. At the other extreme they have been identified with the *singular* names of logic, and accorded a maximum of implication. It is perhaps safer to say that they are indeed slightly descriptive, but only incidentally to their purpose, which is to identify. Thus *John* specifies various individuals, without suggesting any more about them than that they are not women or places (Bosanquet: *Logic*, vol. i., pp. 50, 51).

7

showing a certain "differentia" or characteristic attribute not common to the rest of the genus. The plural of a noun means either (1) its "extension," or (2) the species or kinds it includes. "Material" nouns (*sand, wine*) and some others (*trout, perch, barley*, etc.) take plurals only in the latter sense. If we represent the attributes more or less common to a series of like individuals (aggregates of attributes) by the overlappings in a series of circles, the scope of their class-names (e.g., *horse*) can be shown as follows:—

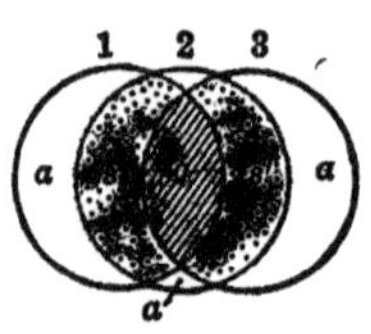

(*the*) *horse* (genus), *g*, attributes essential to all.

barb, or *stallion*, $g + s$ or $g + s'$, generic attributes + specific difference.

a horse, 1, 2, or 3, generic attributes + specific difference + individual traits.

horses, 1, 2, and 3.

We should evidently need more than three individuals to get a plurality of species by the same *ground* of division. With two such species we could say, for example, that *the horses* (*of central Asia*) meant *s* and *s'*.[1] The figure illustrates the fact that as applied to concrete instances any

[1] Note that circle 2 represents an *average* individual. A *typical* individual, with which 'average' is often confused, occurs when there is more than one ground of distinction, as is the case with class-concepts that are popular rather than scientific. Thus since a 'noun' is distinguished by content, form, and function; a 'Frenchman,' by racial stock, native tongue, and citizenship, we have *typical* nouns and Frenchmen. This would be shown by overlapping circles that stand not for aggregates of attributes,

name covers features (*a, a, a*, the "accidents" of logic) that it does not *imply*. This fact affects the uses of adjectives and verbs as well as of nouns, and gives all description in language a fringe of vagueness.

Attribute-names that are nouns by form and function are in grammar called "abstract" nouns. The term is not happy, for it does not accord with the true distinction between abstract and concrete. Any idea, whether of a thing or of an attribute, is abstract when it is thought of apart from the cases in which it is actually experienced. When thought of as realised in objects and instances, it is concrete. Hence the intension of any name is abstract; its extension is concrete. Now these so-called "abstract" nouns have extension or concrete meaning just as much as other nouns: *a whiteness*, *a visitation* are respectively an object and an act. Qualities and events, too, are of various classes, so that their names have like generic and general uses, and regularly take plurals to express their kinds and instances. There is perhaps no harm in calling these "abstract" by their formal intention, since they are the forms used in abstract definitions of the attribute-mean-

---

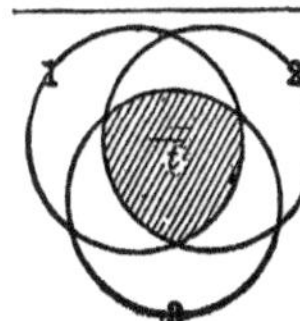

as above, but for aggregates of individuals to which the distinctive attributes *apply;* thus—

1. Words of noun content.
2. Words of noun form.
3. Words of noun function.

t. Typical nouns.

ings.[1] But the true distinction of abstract and concrete, general and particular, refers not to words but to propositions. Books on grammar and logic are apt to confuse their students by talking as if one could take a list of words, apart from any context, and by simple inspection tell which are abstract, general, etc. These terms, however, are in point only when we have assertions to deal with: *a man called here to-day; a man's a man for a' that; faith is assurance of things hoped for; shall he find faith on the earth?* What they mean should be discussed for sentences. At the present point grammar may well enough describe the linguistic devices by which assertions appear as general, concrete, etc., in typical sentence-formulas. But it overshoots the mark in assuming that mere word- and phrase-forms in a sentence hold us down to a single mode of conceiving what it asserts.

A distinct "part of speech" might have been made with the variously designative and quantitative words that mark general features of intension and extension for names. The articles are simply movable prefixes of nouns. For example, *a, an* puts the generic senses of *man, action* in ex-

[1] Infinitives and other verbals are abstract nouns freely formed on the stems of verbs. This formal kinship with words that are "typically" concrete gives them more vividness than the regular "abstract" derivatives; as in *peccāre licet nēminī; to err is human* (cf: *error is human*). English verbals in *-ing* have a sense of continuance not found in the noun-forms identical with their verbs. Thus cf. *a shouting in the distance, a shout in the dark.*

tension to mean the realised but unspecified units *a man, an action.* In certain phrases, however, it has the distributive force of *each;* as in, *two cents a pound; many a man* (each of many men) *had failed.* Cf. *deux fois la semaine. The* commonly specifies an individual. In some languages the definite article is so used redundantly with a proper name; as, ὁ Σωκράτης, *la France, die Briefe des Horaz. The*, again, has with the singular a limited generic use, as in, *the horse is a mammal,* where other languages use a generic article freely, even with abstract nouns and infinitives; as, ἡ ἀρετή, τὸ εἰδέναι; *l'homme est mortel; la beauté; die Zeit steht nie still; das Lesen.* Finally, *the* and its equivalents in other languages serve to put the meaning of adjectives in extension; that is, into the "substantive" use of denoting individuals having, or instances of, their attributes; as in, *how sleep the dead? the sublime and the ridiculous.* Like the articles, such "pronominal" and "limiting" adjectives as *this, my, which, who, anyone, all, some, such, every* express for nouns either an aspect of their extension, or their bearing in the context. Hence although the mind has an acutely discriminative sense of their use, they are hard words to define. "Possessive adjectives" (*my, thy, his,* etc.) might be described geometrically as projections of *I, thou, he,* etc., upon the field of relation.[1] The relations actually expressed with

[1] L. Sütterlin: *das Wesen der Sprachlichen Gebilde,* p. 90.

them vary with the nouns they apply to. In *my answer*, *my discomfort*, *my detractor*, *my fall*, *in my despite*, and many other of their normal uses, these cannot be called "possession" by any stretch of the term. Demonstratives (*this*, *hoc*, *cet*, etc.) designate what is nearer or more remote to the speaker, whether objectively in space and time, or within the context; distributives (*each*, *every*, etc.), designate by the relation of members to a total. The last-named, together with the quantitative words, *all*, *no*, *some*, *any*, *few*, etc., determine the logical "quantity" of a proposition by fixing the extension of its subject. To class these words as adjectives is inept. They take part in the name only by indicating how to think it.

In text-books of logic a proposition that makes its assertion of all the individuals denoted by its subject-noun is called Universal; one making its assertion of part of them only, is Particular. Formal logic, in fact, looks to extension only, both in the subject and in the predicate, which in idiomatic speech is not "quantified." Thus, *brave men are chivalrous* expresses for logic not the relation of subject and attribute that it ordinarily means, but a relation of identity between 'all brave men' and 'some chivalrous beings.' Identity and difference are conventionally shown by diagrams as inclusion and exclusion,[1] thus—

[1] Such figures aim to evade the ambiguities in words. *All*, for example, may mean 'all taken together' (*cunctī*) or 'each and

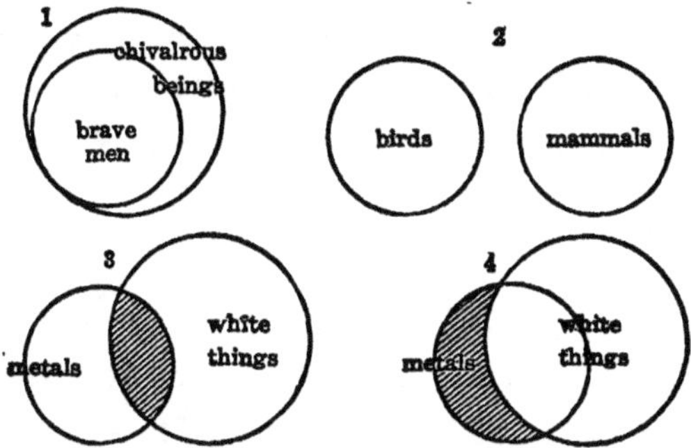

1. Universal affirmative: *All brave men are chivalrous.*
2. Universal negative: *No birds are mammals.*
3. Particular affirmative: *Some metals are white.*
4. Particular negative: *Some metals are not white.*

Not much profit, however, comes of merely describing such artificially "quantified" propositions. Even if it does not betray one into irrelevant quantifying,[1] it leaves untouched the real difficulties of language and thinking, where the question is not how to reason from sentences prearranged into "logical" form, but how to interpret sentences as they naturally come, with the am-

every' (*omnes*), so that one can say both, *all the angles of a triangle equal two right angles*, and *all the angles of a triangle are less than two right angles. Few*, again, has the negative force of 'but few,' so that *few metals are white* (=many metals are not white) would be a particular negative proposition. *A few*, on the other hand, is affirmative. *A few metals are white* would serve for example 3 above. Cf. also, *nothing* (i.e., of all things not one) *is better than honour*, and *half a loaf is better than nothing* (not anything at all).

[1] As where Baynes (*Essay on the New Analytic of Logical Forms*) takes *Great is Diana* as "Some great is all Diana!"

biguities that lurk in idiomatic form. Grammar will clear the way for philosophical thinking, if it leads its pupils to look for the logical character both of words and sentences, not so much to their forms as to their *context*.

Pronouns and numerals are simply common nouns of such meagre intension that their application shifts with the context. A single relation—as of the persons concerned in the discourse, of nearer and farther, of number, etc.—distinguishes their kinds: personal, demonstrative, interrogative, indefinite, relative, cardinal, ordinal, distributive; but within any kind they may divide by further aspects, as where the personals take reflexive and emphatic forms (*myself*, *himself*), distinct forms for different sex (*he*, *she*), or for "conjunctive" and "disjunctive" use (*je*, *moi*; *tu*, *toi*; *il*, *lui*). Since the same word often falls within different classes, one must again beware of classifying the words, instead of their uses within given contexts. Their common labels may here gloss over real differences. Thus of the "personal" pronouns only those of the first and second really designate "persons concerned in the discourse." The third is a sort of neuter person, and its forms are used much like the demonstratives; for example, where they serve as skeleton-subjects, pointing forward to the real subjects: *it is well to speak truth; elle approche, cette mort inexorable.*

Of the three features of inflected nouns,—gender, number, and case,—Gender, except where it distinguishes actual sex, is a purely grammatical figment, marking function rather for the adjective than for the noun. Distinction for actual sex (as between *prince*, *princess*) does not alone give grammatical gender. The latter, in the case of most nouns (especially in French, which lacks the neuter), is purely a matter of formal agreement. English, therefore, has no real gender, since the forms *he*, *she*, *it*, etc., which are conventionally said to show it, always refer to actual or imputed sex, and English names distinguishing sex (*boy*, *girl*; *host*, *hostess*) take no concord for it. Gender in nouns harks back to a primitive distinction in names of things for their felt *value:* as between things of higher and lower order, or between living and inanimate. Hottentots, for example, vary the word *water* as 'masculine' for a 'great water' or river, as 'feminine' for 'water to use' (drinking-water, etc.), and as 'neuter' for the bare name. The so-called masculine, feminine, and neuter of Indo-German speech began in such a twofold value-distinction, including not only that between living and inanimate, but one between men and weaker folk. These classes cut across each other and thereby brought about the threefold division, of which the formal marks spread to all names by analogies partly of value, partly of sound.

Number, as we have seen, has grammatical import for nouns, chiefly as it affects the "quantity" of propositions. In the personal pronouns it may be said to make differences of content. This is evident in languages[1] that have for the dual an "inclusive" form (*I*+*you*) and an "exclusive" one (*I*+*he*). The "trial" gives a form for the three persons singular (*I*+*you*+*he*). *We* and *ye*, of course, are not strictly the plurals of *I* and *thou*, since *we*, for example, is not *I*+*I*+*I*, etc.; but they are felt as such: *we*, as 'I and my party,' etc. In some nouns the plural takes a peculiar use: thus, 'what happened in the *sixties*' refers not to groups of sixty-year units, but to years (*sixty-one*, *sixty-two*, etc.) having *sixty* as a sort of surname, much as in 'what happened to the *Smiths*.' Of the Cases, the nominative is the only one that has strictly noun-function, for the oblique cases, as Sweet remarks, "are really attribute-words, and inflection is practically nothing but a device for turning a noun into an adjective or adverb."[2] Case will therefore come up for notice in the later sections of this chapter.

Predicate and Verb. By function the verb is a word that asserts. It therefore presupposes a subject word as given, except where in flectional forms it includes a subject-element (φέρ-ει, *fer-it*),

[1] Those of the Dravidian family.

[2] *Philolog. Soc. Trans.*, 1875–6, p. 493.

and may stand as at once word and sentence. Assertion—the imputing of truth or falsehood to a logical relation—does not, conversely, require a verb: for many exclamatory words (*splendid! how true! que de fleurs!*) have an assertive force. But since in full assertive sentences finite verbs always fall within the predicate, any distinction between kinds of verb should begin with one between kinds of predicate.

Formal grammar makes out four classes of predicate, which, reduced to their simplest terms, are as follows:—

	Subject	Predicate		
		Verb	Object	Complement
1.	Twilight	falls.	. . .	. . .
	Pompey	is defeated	. . .	. . .
2.	Snow	is	. . .	white.
	Ecgberht	was made	. . .	king.
	A beast	becomes	. . .	fractious.
3.	Caesar	has defeated	Pompey.	. . .
	He	teaches	(1) the dog	. . .
			(2) tricks.	. . .
4.	Teasing	renders	a beast	fractious.
	The Saxons	did make	Ecgberht	king.
	All	would think	her	beautiful.

Of these four predicates, no. 1 requires for its verb neither object-word nor complement; no. 2 requires the complement but not the object; no. 3, the object but not the complement; no. 4, both object and complement. In all four classes the verb itself appears either as one word or as more than one. We have to deal, therefore, with a distribution of meaning, first in the verb, then in the whole predicate; and at each of these junctures we get a classification of verbs.

Verb Content: Copula, Auxiliary, and Notional Verbs. A predicate term must, at the very simplest, express: (1) an idea predicated; (2) the fact of its predication. When single words thus express both content and predicate-function, we have typical verbs, by which, indeed, most ideas of *occurrence* are represented in language.[1] For many other ideas, however, no verbs exist, so that their predication must be expressed analytically by an adjective or noun with a copula-word. If in these cases the copula must be classed as a verb by its function, it evidently differs from typical verbs by the fact that it does not of itself make a predicate term. Such content as it has adds but little to that term's notional complex.

[1] The fact that occurrences are commonly named by words of verb "habit" has led some writers to make out a distinct category of verb meaning. Wundt calls this "Zustand" (see note, p. 88), Sweet (*New English Grammar*, p. 89), "changing attribute." But either of these terms must be applied so loosely (compare, for the latter, *candēre*, 'be white;' *lie, stand, shine, remain*) as to have no descriptive value.

This difference has already appeared within the copula-word *be*, which sometimes affirms a content-idea of actual existence[1] (compare, *we be twelve brethren* with *the powers that be*). At bottom it is simply the difference between naming and relating, and gives: (1) notional verbs, which have a content adequate to serve as predicate-ideas (as, *exist, fall, shout, take, approve*), and (2) relating verbs, which have as content merely general categories of sense, within which they serve to predicate a noun or adjective complement.

In statements of universal import (such as *silence is golden; twice two is four; fortūna cæca est; inimīca inter sē sunt lībera cīvitās et rex*) *is, are* and their equivalents are perhaps pure copulas, particles that simply assert without implying anything as to what is asserted. But in common statements of particular fact the various forms of *be, esse, être*, etc., express for the asserted fact its setting in time, and its character as actual, contingent, etc.; as, *Cain* *was* *wroth; the Douglas* *is* *present; to lose thee* *were* *to lose myself; il n'y a personne qui ne* *soit* *pauvre; nōmine, non potestāte,* *fuit* *rex; quālis* *sit* *animus, animus nescit; dōnec* *eris* *fēlīx, multōs numerābis amīcōs.* A minimum of content, therefore, is carried even by the typical copula-verbs. Next to these in comparative

[1] Not to mention its idiomatic senses, such as *he had been* (gone) *the rounds.*

emptiness of content are certain verbs expressing a transition to, a causing of, or other general relation to what is specified by a predicate adjective or noun. Such "verbs of incomplete predication" appear in *became king, turn pale, fall sick, grow old, went mad, seems pleased, continued running, proved true, set free, render null.* In all these cases notional verbs carry but little more than copula meaning. Indeed, if the true predicate of a sentence lies where it makes the actual advance in thought, any notional verb may subordinate its sense to the point of being felt as that predicate's copula. This is specially evident where its content has been somewhat anticipated. Thus in, *what ails him? he has jaundice; they were prompt,—they came on the run, has* and *came* are virtual copulas. Such a weakening in verb-content may answer to a different grouping of ideas. Whereas in *he stood firmly* the 'firmness' is referred to 'his standing,' in *he stood firm* it is referred to 'him.'

To the verb as the word that makes assertion—the "live word" as it is called in Chinese—attach various sense-categories that are involved in its reference to given reality. Some of these have grammatical names—voice, mood, tense—and in fully inflected verbs have their distinctions expressed by changes of form. For other verbs such distinctions are wholly or partly expressed by phrases made up of their noun and adjective forms with the copula, or with auxiliary verbs, that is, copula-verbs that as such are limited to this use. Thus in πέφανται, *monstrātum est*, *has been shown*, the Greek uses an inflected notional word where Latin uses one, and English two, auxiliaries. Since it is only by comparison with inflected verbs that such phrases are classed as "forms" of the notional verb, instead of as copula and complement, the division of such predicates as *snow is white*, *Pompey is defeated* into the two classes shown above is merely conventional. An auxiliary, like other copula-verbs, has a content of its own, but in its auxiliary use this fades to a mere reminiscence, colouring the assertion that it introduces. Thus the much discussed choice between *shall* and *will* arises from their respective content-notions of 'necessity' and 'intention.' These make *you shall, he shall* express the speaker's promise or prediction of another's action, and hence imply some authority or compulsion on the former's part. *I shall* expresses mere futurity, since in promising his own future action the speaker asserts no special authority. *I will* expresses volition, which is weakened or lost in *you will, he will*, since one does not readily think of the speaker as asserting an intention in another's mind. English is rich in auxiliary verbs, and its six typical ones show their essential features:—

VERB	CONTENT	USED AS AUXILIARY TO FORM:—
be	exist	(1) passive voice—*is taken;* (2) "continuous" tenses—*is going;* (3) phrases with obligatory force—*I am to go.*
do	perform effect	(1) imperative mood—*do be quiet;* (2) present and preterit tense phrases, especially in questions and other inverted constructions, or in emphatic assertion—*do you know? never did I see; I did do it.*
have	hold	"perfect" tenses—*mine eyes have seen it.*
shall	owe, be bound	future tenses—*I shall lead; should* forms (1) "preterit future" tense—*it was evident that I should see him;* (2) "conditional" mood—*should he stir, hold him.*
will	wish, intend	future tenses; *would* is used (1) like *should*, and to express the matter asserted (2) as what might be expected—*primitive man would give names;* (3) as customary—*he would drop in of an evening.*
may	be permitted	contingent mood—*he may rue it. Might* here expresses the matter asserted as contrary to fact or expectation—*you might apologise; O might I see that day!*

Auxiliary verbs are most handy expressive devices. *Do*, for example, can carry almost all the grammatical adjustment of verb constructions, leaving its principal verb to carry the specific content without a change of form or even of word-order. Cf. *spake he?* with *did he speak?*

Thus far we have had to do with a distribution of meaning between words representing copula and content of phrased simple predicates. "Simple" we call these predicates because to withdraw from one of them its notional complement would be to leave its assertion not thinkably complete. Thus, to say *Ecgberht became; haste makes*, without further words (*king, waste*) leaves a sensation much like that of missing a step downstairs. The simplest predicate, therefore, requires that a content adequate to make an explicit advance in thought, be carried either: (1) by a notional verb alone; (2) by a noun or adjective with the copula; or (3) by a semi-notional copula-word with a complement. Any further development of predicate-content calls for "modifiers," which, strictly speaking, render the predicate no longer simple. One kind of modifier, however, is so knit with a verbal idea, that grammarians have taken it as giving further classes of simple predicate (classes 3 and 4, p. 107). This term is the Object. Many verbs as *push, like, possess,* express an act, process, feeling, or relation as directed upon some person or thing. Logically, this notion of the recipient of an act, etc., is, like that of its agent, related to it as subject to attribute, and in inflected languages such verbs have in the "passive voice" a set of forms to express their content obversely for the recipient as grammatical subject, with the agent expressed adverbially, if at all. Thus for *prōvidentia mundum administrat* we may have *prōvidentiā mundus administrātur.* School grammars, therefore, attempt to classify all notional verbs as either Transitive, taking a direct object; or Intransitive, expressing an act, feeling, state, etc., as self-complete. It would be more accurate so to classify not the verbs themselves, but their

8

uses, since "transitive" verbs may express their content "absolutely," that is, as conceived apart from the object involved (*he let the bandits kill and steal*); "intransitive" ones often develop special transitive uses (*to walk one's horse; to cry one's eyes red; to talk oneself hoarse; A lover's eyes will gaze an eagle blind; to look daggers; festīnāre fugam*) and many verbs, as *timat*, 'he fears,' 'he is afraid,' freely take either use. Even with this restriction, we cannot view transitiveness as inhering exclusively in the verb, since in analytic speech it is often expressed for the verb by a particle; as in, *she looked at him; he dreams of empire.*[1] Many verbs, though expressing a self-complete action or state, take a so-called "cognate" object,—one that simply extends the verb-idea into the object-construction; as, *servitūtem servīre; to fight the good fight;* πίπτειν πέσημα, 'to fall a fall' (Cf. Chinese *ch'ang*[4] *i*[2] *ch'ang*[4], *tso*[4] *i*[2] *tso*[4], etc., 'sing a sing,' 'sit a sit,' etc.).[2] Perhaps on the analogy of this construction we have in English *foot it; lord it; whether the charmer sinner it or saint it,*—where the formal object specialises a verbal use of words with noun "habit."

[1] The particle here is not adverbial, as when it supplements a transitive use: *shut to the door* or *shut the door to.* A difference of sense may depend on where the particle is felt to attach: cf. *he laughed at-that moment; he laughed-at the idea; John was sent-for; James was sent for-John.*

[2] In Greek this cognate object is sometimes represented by a neuter adjective qualifying it; as, μεγάλα ἁμαρτάνειν, 'to commit great faults.'

The distinction of transitive and intransitive, therefore, though beginning with a definition of verb-content, brings up at the mere question whether or not an object-word is present, and has little descriptive value outside of obvious cases. Object and complement constructions divide not so much by a line as by a neutral belt in which they merge. In *the dog is taught tricks* the "retained object" shows no logical difference from a complement, as in *the dog is bred true;* while the "adverbial object" distinguished in *the opening measures ten feet; the land totals six acres*, is a mere courtesy title. A clear object-relation obtains only where something is the goal of movement. It is but one of many relations by which acts are defined, and in many cases the true relation is only obscured by calling the defining noun an "object." What we actually have in any predicate is a sense-complex that may break up quite diversely in the process of matching it with words. The kind and number of its resulting words is partly a question of vocabulary (we have *put to death* or *kill*, but *put to sleep* or —?), partly one of coherence: *amātus eram* is two words, *amābam* one, because *-bam*, *-bas*, *-bat* (originally bhu̯ām, 'I grew') do not, like *eram*, etc., shift their position or occur apart; and in "separable" forms (*er fängt an, ich fuhr fort; I sat out the night*—cf. *er ist fortgefahren; I outlived my aunt*) the verb varies between one word and more. Grammar, therefore, gets little profit from a rigorous effort at labelling "kinds of verb." It will keep to more fruitful work by showing simply what in predicate-formulas are free elements, and what are fixed.

VERB FORM. If language were truly systematic, one would expect the verb as the kernel of the predicate to have a consistent scheme of forms to express economically certain general categories of sense—intensity, reversal, passivity, etc.—for the same words. Some of these categories—voice, mood, and tense—actually give inflectional schemes, but a comparison, say, of the Greek and the English verb, shows that their distinctions are made with a wasteful number of forms,[1] while other distinctions are made too sporadically to establish any scheme at all. For example, we have but irregular traces of causative forms in *drench* (make drink), *fell* (make fall), *lay* (make lie); of intensive ones in *sculpō*, 'carve, hollow out' (cf. *scalpō*, 'scratch, scrape'),

[1] Any count of forms, however, is apt to be misleading as to the actual amount of speech-material that must be mastered in learning their distinctions. Thus to say that an English verb has only six or seven forms as against 507 in Greek is to ignore not only such mood and tense phrases as answer to the Greek, but such as make the distinctions between *writes*, *is writing*, *does write*. Again, the 507 Greek forms (as counted by Curtius: *das griechische Verbum*, p. 5) result in part quite systematically. Given the present active and middle of λύω, and an inserted σ will give all its future active and middle, while an inserted θη in the future middle gives all its future passive.

bedeck, *besmear*, etc.; while distinctive gnomic forms for abstract assertion do not occur, although they would avert real ambiguities, as by showing whether *boys are troublesome* means that boys happen now to be giving trouble, or that troublesomeness is their fixed trait.

(1) VOICE. Transitiveness in a verb—its expression of an act, process, feeling, or relation as directed upon a person or thing—gives rise to the distinction called Voice. When, by a verb's form or construction, the agent of its act, or the one that has its asserted feeling or relation, is expressed as its subject, we have the Active voice; when the recipient, or the one towards which the feeling or relation is borne, is expressed as its subject, we have the Passive. Between active and passive we can have a Reflexive or Middle voice, in which agent and recipient are the same. Historically, the passive has in a number of languages been developed from the reflexive. French and Italian still make frequent use of the latter construction for the former; as in, *cela se laisse dire; la nature se divise en deux règnes; les événements se sont vite oubliés; quésto líbro si lêgge; quêlle côse si facévano.* With these three sense-constructions, and three corresponding sets of forms, one might expect nine cases of voice-distinction, since, what with sense-developments and sense-survivals, word-forms characteristic of each voice occur with the

meanings of the other two. In fact, it will prove convenient to tabulate these nine cases, and discuss them in their order, noting matters that complicate one's analysis as they arise:—

Form		Verb	Construction: Subject	Construction: Object	Description
Form	Active	1. He *fells* the tree.	agent	recipient	active
		2. They *bathe* in pools.	agent & recipient	——	intrans. reflexive
		3. Tortoise *eats* like veal.	recipient	——	neuter passive
	Reflexive	4. er *freut sich*, 'he rejoices' (lit., delights himself).	bearer of the feeling	formal?	reflex. intrans.
		5. *ἐτράποντο πρὸς λῃστείαν*, 'they turned (themselves) to piracy.	agent & recipient	——	middle
		5. *ὁ δῆμος τίθεται νόμους*, 'the people make (themselves) laws.'	agent & indirect recipient	direct recip.	middle
		6. le livre *se vend*, 'the book sells.'	recipient	formal?	reflexive passive
		6. *ἀδικήσομαι*, 'I shall be wronged.'	(recipient)	——	reflexive passive
	Passive	7. The tree *is felled.*	recipient	——	passive
		8. ferrō *accingor*, 'I gird myself with my sword.'	agent & recipient	——	passive reflexive
		9. dēteriōra *sequor*, 'I follow the worse.'	(agent)	recipient	deponent

Example 1 is typical of the active voice. Instead of the agent-and-recipient relation between subject and object, we may have any other relation felt to be analogous; as in, *Lot beheld Zoar, the winnings approximate ten dollars.* The analogy, in fact, is often so remote as to amount to a grammatical fiction. Such is the case, for example, in *dētrimenta rīdet*, 'he laughs at losses;' *I fear Varro*, and in constructions with adverbial or cognate objects (*the winnings totalled five counts; he shall die the death*), where the active voice is remarked only when a corresponding passive might be called for. In such impersonal verbs as *pudet, piget, taedet, paenitet*, the agent may be thought of as an implied "cognate" subject. Examples 2 and 3 show active forms with reflexive and passive meanings. English has a number of verbs, normally transitive, which may thus express intransitively a specialised reflexive or passive sense; as in, *he girded for combat; corn sells cheap; will the meat keep?* On the other hand, *bask* and *busk*, in which *sk* stands for an old reflexive pronoun, have almost lost their reflexive meaning.

Since any transitive verb may take a reflexive pronoun (*myself, himself, oneself*, etc.) to express its act, etc., as directed upon its subject,[1] the literal reflexive construction (*he bathes himself*) is merely a special case of the active voice. Hence the only advantage in distinguishing a reflexive voice is when this construction expresses an intransitive or passive meaning, as in examples 4 and 6, or when the verb takes special forms for it, as in the Greek middle (examples 5 and 6). In *ils s'aiment*,

[1] Cf. also *own*, which in *he cooked his own dinner* adds reflexive force to the verb.

etc., the French uses it further to express a sort of Reciprocal voice.

Example 7 is typical of the passive. It expresses a transitive notion in which an agent, though not specified, is implied, whereas the corresponding intransitive in *the tree falls* implies nothing as to any cause.[1] Verbs made transitive by a particle as *stare at, think of, rely on,* may express their sense passively, like other transitives; as, *one hates to be stared at; his word is relied on.* Examples 8 and 9 show passive forms with reflexive and active meaning. The passive of certain intransitive verbs expresses their action as accomplishing itself; as *παρεσκεύασται*, 'preparation has been made;' *curritur*, 'there is a running;' *pūgnātur*, 'a fight is on,' *itur*, 'some one goes.' The construction (here impersonal, with implied "cognate" subject) proceeds from the original reflexive meaning of the passive.[2]

(2) Mood. The speaker's concern with what is said we have remarked as that which gives the sentence its distinctive value as assertion, wish, supposal, etc. Where this subjective element is expressed in a verb we get grammatical Mood. Something of mood lies in the very nature of a

[1] The intransitive sense does not, of course, *exclude* a cause or even an agent, which may be further expressed for it; as, *the tree falls by its own weight; he died by the hand of a traitor.*

[2] Allen and Greenough: *New Latin Grammar*, p. 120.

verb, for its implied copula makes the reference of thought to reality that distinguishes ideas applied to the world of fact from ideas merely "entertained." Mood at its simplest, then, imputes to the content of a sentence or clause some relation to truth. This relation is called in logic the "modality" of a proposition, viz., that by which it is distinguished as asserting (or denying) the possibility, impossibility, contingency, or necessity of its content. Kant made out three "modes" of assertion: (1) that of *possibility*, which gives "problematical" propositions (*dogs may think*); (2) that of *actuality*, which gives "assertory" propositions (*this dog notices separate qualities*); (3) that of *necessity*, which gives "apodeictic" propositions (*if dogs think, they must analyse*). Propositions, in this view, show degrees of "downrightness." Thus, according to Bosanquet[1] "apodeictic" ones are the most "assertive," because they make explicit the conditions subject to which their truth necessarily follows; and assertory ones come next, since their reference to truth, though not called for by logical consistency, is direct, whereas in problematic ones it is indirect. Problematic ones, indeed, express this reference directly, but do so with a reservation that shows it to be subject to unexpressed conditions or transitions. Thus the judgment 'dogs may think' derives whatever "assertiveness" it has from the truth

[1] *Logic*, i., p. 388 ff.

of the other two judgments viz., that 'this dog analyses,' and that 'analysis is one factor in thinking.' The degree of certainty here is conceived as a matter not of mere feeling, but of insight into the logical bearings of ideas.

Beginning with Gottfried Hermann in 1801,[1] grammarians have applied Kant's modal categories in whole or in part to descriptive schemes for mood-syntax. Uses of the subjunctive, for example, they explain as resulting from one comprehensive subjunctive-meaning, either possibility, or uncertainty, or 'Nichtwirklichkeit,' or the like. It is of course not fair to object that such schemes are too abstruse and technical for a plain man to recognise as describing his talk. Language abounds in niceties to which plain people are quite alive in their talk without having the analytic power to define them. But it would be alien to what we find elsewhere in language, if

[1] Hermann's work (*De Emendanda Ratione Grammaticae Graecae*) assigned the indicative to 'actuality,' the optative to 'subjective possibility' (*possibilitas cogitata*), the subjunctive to 'objective possibility' (*possibilitas per ipsarum rerum condicionem*), the imperative to 'subjective necessity,' and the verbal in -τέος to 'objective necessity.' This scheme was variously developed for Greek moods by Matthiae, Dissen, and Thiersch; and then applied to other languages, as by Zumpt to Latin, by Jakob Grimm to German, and by Mätzner to French and English. See W. G. Hale: 'A Century of Metaphysical Syntax,' *Proceedings of the Congress of the St. Louis Exposition*, iii. (1904), and 'The Heritage of Unreason in Syntactical Method,' *Proceedings of the Classical Association of England*, v. (1907).

formal classes, like these of mood, should prove to have each a single abstract meaning which covers its particular instances. In words and case-forms the development of particular meanings has proceeded less by any logical use of categories than by associations felt between one immediate instance and another; and the same is likely to have been true of moods. Moreover, the *understood* relation to truth that gives "modality" is something narrower and more retrospective than the bare reference to fact that figures in mood. For example, mood expresses not only the *logical notion* of possibility that a speaker arrives at by deliberately viewing his assertion apart from the conditions that make it valid, but a *feeling* as to its possibility arising from his mere inability to grasp the conditions. The psychological features of conviction, misgiving, reserve, enter equally with the logical into its distinctions. Mood, that is, expresses *how* the speaker conceives his assertion, without intimating *why* he so conceives it.

So far as relation to fact is concerned, we might, then, think to replace their logical scheme of the possible, the real, and the necessary with a psychological one of doubt, belief, and certainty. Actual speech, however, gets along here with two distinctions, so that as respects fact a statement is either downright or non-committal. If it is true enough to be acted upon, the speaker is satisfied to assert it. Assertion, after all, cannot be more than true, and a 'mood of certainty' is sufficiently supplied by *must* and a few phrases of conviction, such as *of course, to be sure,* etc. The distinction of downright and non-committal mood—'fact-mood' and 'thought-mood'[1]—is made in our languages by the indicative and the subjunctive. Thus in indirect discourse Modern German, like Old English, can transpose the matter reported into a non-committal key, as it were: 'Hans *hat* kein Geld'—Hans sagt, dass er kein Geld *habe.*' Various uses of the Latin subjunctive show typically the speaker's reservation that makes it assert what is simply contemplated or possible:—the "potential" in *hīc quaerat quispiam,* 'here some one *may ask;*' the "concessive" in *fuerint pertinācēs,* '*granted* they were obstinate;' the subjunctive in "less vivid future condition"—*quod sī quis deus mihi largiātur,* '*should* some god grant me this;' that in "final" clauses—*scrībēbat ōrātiōnēs quās aliī dīcerent,* 'he wrote speeches for others to speak;' and that in causal clauses which assign a reason on the authority of another—*māter īrāta est quia non redierim,* 'mother is angry because I did n't return.' In certain uses it seems to differentiate as thought from fact what really differs as general from particular. Thus in *memoria minuitur, nisi eam exerceās,* 'memory becomes impaired, unless one *exercise* it,' the sub-

[1] These terms are from Henry Sweet's *New English Grammar,* Part i., p. 106.

junctive points to what is in mind as not an act but a kind of act, and makes the thought an abstract one about 'memory without exercise.' So in "clauses of characteristic"—*sapientia est ūna, quae maestitiam pellat*—it marks the expression, not of a concrete instance, but of a defining attribute.

No consistent scheme of fact-mood and thought-mood, however, is actually carried out. Here as elsewhere in language, the working of analogy was bound to cut across logical lines. For example, the Latin subjunctive, from expressing *characteristic* result—'wisdom is such a thing as to dispel sadness'—passed into clauses expressing *instances* of result; as in, *effēcit ut īmperātor mitterētur.* In questions and suppositions, where assertion of fact is precluded in the nature of the case, the fact-mood (indicative) may be used for vividness; as in, *if he is right, I am wrong.* Supposition viewed as contrary to fact is distinguished not by mood, but by past tense—remote time passing into remote likelihood; as, *if it were so* (cf. *if it be so*). Mood and tense, indeed, are at various points bound to overlap. Thus the future tense, expressing what is not yet realised, becomes dubitative in the Scottish—*ye 'll no be o' this country, freend?* (=I suppose you are not, etc.)—and imperative in military commands—*you will report at headquarters*—where the simple statement of another's future act implies an authority *directing* that he so act.

But the final objection to modality as a norm for mood lies in the circumstance that moods have developed in speech as much by people's *emotional* concern with what they say as by their view of its relation to fact. Will and wish gave rise to distinct moods,[1] and where these prompt the utterance its status as fact is but indirectly in point. Command and question—*take thy face hence! shall I budge?*—charge the thought with an expectation that it will be realised as fact by an act or answer of the hearer. Exclamation and wish—*what a fall was there! perish the thought!*—stress it as a matter of feeling. An *indirect* imputation as to fact it may indeed get, just as in oblique cases we have indirect naming.[2]

The expression of this concern of the speaker with what he says is not limited to verbal mood. It may, of course, be put into a separate assertion; as, 'that Ishmael live *is my desire.*' In exclamation—*Hannibal ad portās!*—it is conveyed by the force and quality of the tones in which the whole sentence is uttered. In question—*are you ready? you are ready?*—it appears in the word-order or in

[1] These moods, of course, become specialised to show certain relations to fact, as where the Greek optative either (as in ἔλθοι ἄν, 'he might go') makes a point of the speaker's neutrality, or (as in εἰ γένοιτο, 'if it should happen'—cf. ἐὰν γένηται, 'if it happen') expresses a remoter likelihood than would appear from the subjunctive.

[2] Thus in *John's gospel* the genitive means not 'John in a relation' but 'a relation to John,' which is here an attribute of *gospel.*

a rising intonation. In any sentence it may be shown by parenthetic words—*perhaps*, *doubtless*, *indeed*, *happily*, *probably*,—which point a reflection not upon any one term, but upon the sentence as a whole. The early practice of repeating negatives through a sentence without regard to their cancelling one another, cast the whole utterance into a "negative mood:"[1] *he nevere yet no vileinye ne sayde in al his lyf, unto no maner wight.* In auxiliary verbs we soon pass from distinctions of the speaker's concern that are properly modal, to those in which it is merely part of the asserted content. Thus in *take it away!* the cutting edge of the utterance is its appeal to be acted on,—an appeal that becomes indirect in *you must take it.*

It must be evident that the problem of describing mood is peculiarly complicated. To begin with, one must bear in mind the distinction just made, that modal force consists not in *any* expressed element of the speaker's concern, but only in that which imparts to the sentence or clause its expressive value. We have no 'desiderative' mood in *scripturiō*, 'I want to write,' for the speaker's wish is here stated as a fact; but in *ut scrīberem!* his wish is what energises the speech-material into this form, and becomes modal. Where we have auxiliaries, in which the subjective element unites with copula function, we

[1] In the Dravidian tongues a negative mood is distinguished for verbs.

may hesitate to say which the value-relation leads through: that is, whether in *do, may, should, is to, can, must, ought,* etc., we really have 'emphatic,' 'permissive,' 'dubitative,' 'cohortative,' and 'compulsive' moods, or shades of feeling presented through the fact-mood. Furthermore, the *expression* of modal force is called mood, only when it inheres in verb-forms. Hence what is sought in any descriptive scheme for the moods is either: (1) to fix upon kinds of modal force and then classify the verb-forms for each; or (2) to begin with the sets of modal forms, and then classify their forces. The first procedure would meet trouble in the circumstance that kinds of feeling vary from one another by no such steps as divide tones in a scale. Thus imperative force shades imperceptibly from bare acquiescence, through consent, suggestion, request, and entreaty, to command. What grammar actually does is to begin with the types of mood-form—which, of course, answer to distinctions of concern broadly taken: that is, with indicative, subjunctive, etc.,—and then to classify the uses of each. Since these uses do not follow as particular meanings from general ones, present work in this field aims simply to ascertain the earliest forces in each mood, and to trace their extension. Professor Hale, for example, puts the problem thus:—

"We are, then, to endeavour to find the force of the subjunctive in this or that concrete example, going ultimately through the whole gamut. The result will be a certain number of constructions, which will probably be reducible to a much smaller number of families, that is, applications of a given force to a number of uses. The forces seen in these families will constitute the leading forces of the mood. So much being accomplished, it is possible that we may then be able, by detecting natural associations of meaning here and there, to determine the probable ways in which these various leading forces came to attach themselves successively to a mood which had originally but a single force. We shall then have reached a rational and satisfactory understanding of the whole, a mood-*system*."[1]

Now where a given modal force—e.g., the 'volitive'—can really be followed through the uses of such a historic type of form as the subjunctive, there is, of course, a scientific gain. But on its formal side the continuity of a mood is apt to be imperfect. Thus the optative, which in Greek has its own inflection, is in Latin merged in the subjunctive; and the subjunctive has in English verbs dwindled to a scattering of forms for the passive and the third person singular active. *I urge that we go* can be said to show the subjunctive only by analogy with *I urge that he go*. Certain

[1] W. G. Hale: 'Grammatical Nomenclature with Especial Reference to Mood-Syntax' (*Publ. of the Modern Language Association of America*, June, 1911).

forces, again, as inflected speech grows analytic, pass from mood-forms to auxiliaries, so that Hale, for example, is led to study "uses of the subjunctive" in *shall*. If, then, one takes as the "leading forces" of a mood those that define themselves in its early history, and can be traced through languages of the same stock, one will fix upon force-categories that are both prominent and identified with unequivocal forms only in the early period. For describing English subjunctive uses we should thus have a set of labels that we had come by from an interest less in what present English shows than in its antecedents and analogies in other tongues. It would occur to nobody to see a volitive subjunctive in *I desire that he come* and not a volitive infinitive in *I desire him to come*, unless he had in mind *ut veniat* and *qu'il vienne*. Any such force, moreover, is in itself so unstable a shade of feeling, that its label can be applied to concrete instances only by reckoning in the meaning of whole contexts. Here one is continually betrayed into assigning the force of a whole word-group to a single modal form within it.[1] Thus Hale cites *te hortor ut maneās, ich will dass du mir gebest* for 'volitive,' and *expectat dum defluat, richtet nicht vor der Zeit, bis der Herr komme* for 'anticipatory,' subjunctives.[2] In the upshot we seem pressed to conclude: (1) that it is profitable to recognise dif-

[1] See E. P. Morris: *op. cit.*, pp. 210–212.

[2] *The School Review*, June, 1911, pp. 374, 375.

ferences of mood only where there are modal distinctions of form; (2) that we should approach the study of a mood in a given language with an undivided interest in what is characteristic of that language: that is, with a caution against emphasising parallels between its uses and those of other tongues or of its own bygone stages; (3) that in each language we need classes of mood-use drawn less from vague categories of modal force than from the *kinds of context* in which a mood occurs. This means describing types of clause, either by meaning, by form, or, perhaps better still, by both. The degree of modal likeness thereby disclosed between different tongues we can then make question of, without a misgiving that the question has been begged.[1]

(3) TENSE. Since in recounting anything our assertions follow an order of occurrences, words that assert naturally bear distinctions to delimit

[1] If modal force is no more a matter of mood-forms than of their context, the current belief that the English subjunctive is disappearing calls for a remark. It is true that the label 'subjunctive' applies now to but few forms in English, and that these suggest literary or cultivated use—which some people think is disappearing. But the "force" associated with it is in no danger of loss, since in each case the contingency, reserve, or whatever shade of 'thought-mood' it stands for, appears in an auxiliary, a conjunction, or in the clause as a whole: thus, *decide nothing until he come; so to act that each to-morrow find us farther than to-day; murder though it have no tongue, will out; be it never so humble, there's no place like home; whatever the word be; ask nothing more than that he obey; I fear lest she lose the path; it is well that a young man bear the yoke.*

their content in point of time,—the distinctions, that is, of Tense. Time as marked by tense is of course only relative: past, present, and future being reckoned as such from the moment of speaking. Having indicated, however, a time before or after that of speaking, one may go on to indicate times as before or after that spoken of; and since a past or future may be further indicated as near or remote, one might have, at least theoretically, a dozen tenses for these relative points of time. Moreover, any act or occurrence may be viewed with respect to the time not only *at* which, but *during* which, it takes place. In the former view, it is expressed, regardless of its actual duration, as if falling at an instantaneous point. Such 'point tenses'[1] appear in, *you touch the button; the guard will sleep below; Semiramis built Babylon.* In the latter view, an occurrence may be expressed solely as at some stage of its duration: as beginning, going on, or finished. For example, the two tenses of Hebrew primarily distinguish the action simply as complete or incomplete,—though with the help of context they serve indirectly to assign it to past, present, or future. In the languages familiarly studied, verb-forms which express a durative aspect of an act or occurrence, express also its historical time; as, *scribēbat, écrivait, he was writing.* The accompanying tabular "Scheme of Tenses"

[1] The term is suggested by Sweet: *New English Grammar*, vol. i., p. 102.

shows the distinctions of tense that are found in these languages.

The annexed scheme by no means exhausts the distinctions of tense that are theoretically possible. For example, we might have forms which delimited the time from not one but two times of comparison. We should then have, say, two tense-forms for *he was going to write*, one of which should mean that he now has, the other that he as yet has not, written. Such an expression as *he has intended to write* shows a sort of twofold tense, for it makes out the intention as past, but the writing as still future. Furthermore, an assertion may be made absolutely, or without reference to historical time at all. Thus in abstract or general statements—*man is mortal; birds fly*—the verb is really tenseless, although it is formally in the present. Since each language has but a limited number of tense-forms, any one of them is apt to serve for more than one tense-distinction. We shall therefore pass in review the tense-names commonly used, referring to the table for the distinctions they cover:—

i. The Present means, as a 'point' tense, that the act or occurrence *now takes place* (sense 6 above); as a 'durative' tense, that it is *now going on* (sense 6*b*). It is also a 'gnomic' tense, asserting what is true at any time; as in, *minōra dī neglegunt*, 'the gods *disregard* trifles;' *twice two is four.* The gnomic present merges into an iterative use, expressing current habit; as in, *I take a walk before breakfast.* In Greek and Latin the progressive present (6*b*) may take on an implication that the act not only is not, but *is not to be* completed. It is then a 'conative' present, expressing attempted action; as in, πείθουσι ὑμᾶς, 'they are trying to persuade you.' This use is sometimes developed from an inceptive present (6*a*); as in, *dēnsōs fertur in hostīs*, 'he starts (unsuccessfully) to rush into the thick of the foe.' With an adverbial expression of past time, the present may cover senses 5*b* and 6*b*, expressing the act as continuing from the past into the present; as in, κεῖνον ἰχνεύω πάλαι, 'I have long been (and still am) tracking him;' *tē jamdūdum hortor;*[1] *il est ici depuis une semaine; er ist schon zehn Jahr Soldat.* The 'historical' present, recounting past events as if present, is assumed for vivid effect. In English and German, which lack the future tense (and sometimes for vividness in other languages), the present often supplies its place; as in, *ich gehe morgen auf die Jagd; I go hunting to-morrow.*

ii. The Past is more accurately distinguished as either 'preterit' or 'imperfect.' The Preterit (in Greek Grammar, the Aorist) expresses simply past occurrence (sense 2); as, ἔγραψε, *écrivit*, 'upon

[1] Here "the English states the beginning and leaves the continuance to be inferred, while the Latin states the continuance and leaves the beginning to be inferred" (Allen and Greenough: *New Latin Grammar*, p. 294). Cf. *I am still* (and have long been) *tracking him.*

SCHEME OF TENSES.

TIME OF COMPARISON:	PAST					PRESENT			FUTURE	
	anterior to past		*anterior to fut. in past*	*future in the past*	*immediate past*		*immediate future*	*past in the future*		*impending in the future*
	1	2	3	4	5	6	7	8	9	10
"POINT":	had written eut écrit	wrote écrivit	would hav written	vould write crirait	has written	writes	is about to write	will have written	will write	will be going to write
DURATIVE:— (*a*) *Inceptive:*	——	[began writing]	——	vould begin writing]	——	[begins writing]	——	——	[will begin writing]	——
(*b*) *Progressive:*	had been writing	was writing écrivait	would have been writi	'ould be writing	has been writing	is writing	is about to be writing	will have been writing	will be writing	will be going to be writing
(*c*) *Perfect:*	——	had written avait écrit	——	vould have written	——	has written (has the act completed)	is about to have written	——	will have written	will be going to have written

'Inceptive' or 'inchoative' forms, as *calēscer* ow warm,' *labāscere*, 'begin to totter,' do not occur with many verbs, and are therefore classed not as tenses, but as distinct derivative v So also are 'iterative' forms—as *cantitāre*, 'to sing again and again'—distinguishing the action as repeated or customary.

arriving *he wrote.*' The Greek aorist of verbs asserting a state or condition, generally expresses entrance into that state (sense 2*a*); as, ἐβασίλευσα, 'I became king.' The aorist sometimes occurs for senses 5 and 1, where we should expect perfect and pluperfect; as, ἐτράποντο ἐς τὸν Πάνορμον, ὅθενπερ ἀνηγάγοντο (whence they [had] set sail). It has also a gnomic use, implying either that what once happened always happens in like cases, or that what never did happen, never does (cf. *Faint heart ne'er w o n fair lady*). Greek, however, like English, commonly expresses general truths by the present. The aorist regularly implies a single or sudden occurrence, where the gnomic present would imply duration.

The Imperfect expresses the act or occurrence as going on in past time (sense 2*b*); as, ἔγραφε, *scribēbat, écrivait, he was writing.* Like the present, it sometimes has an iterative force, expressing (in Greek with ἄν) a past habit; as in, διηρώτων ἄν αὐτούς, 'I would ask them;' *ita cēnsēbat*, 'he used to think so.' In Greek and Latin it has a 'conative' use, sometimes merging into the inceptive sense *2a;* as in, 'Αλόννησον ἐδίδου, 'he offered (tried to give) Halonnesus;' *sēdābant tumultus*, 'they tried to quell the seditions;' *veniēbant*, 'they were setting about coming.' With an adverbial expression pointing to anterior time, it sometimes in Latin and Greek combines senses 1*b* and 2*b*, expressing the continuance of a previous action into the given past time; as in, *iam dūdum flēbam*, 'I had long been weeping;' *il y était depuis longtemps.*

English and German verbs have but one past form, which is normally a preterit, though it has imperfect uses; as in, *while I read, he wrote; Scottish kings were crowned at Scone; ich war schon zehn Jahr Soldat.*

iii. The Future expresses occurrence in time to come (sense 9). It may be progressive (sense 9*b*); and sometimes has a gnomic use; as in, ἀνὴρ ὁ φεύγων καὶ πάλιν μαχήσεται, 'he that fights and runs away, will live to fight another day.' It may have the modal force of an imperative; as, *faciēs ut sciam*, '(you will) let me know.' Greek, Latin, and French use it in a dependent clause expressing future occurrence where English often uses the present, if the futurity is expressed in the main clause; thus, *nātūram sī sequēmur, nūnquam aberrābimus*, 'if we *follow* nature, we never *shall go* astray;' *vous direz ce qu'il vous plaira*, 'you *shall say* whatever you *please*.'

iv. The Perfect normally expresses the occurrence as now finished (sense 6*c*); as, γέγραφα, *scripsit, I have written* (my writing is now done). This is the 'perfect definite;' but since an act now finished must have taken place in past time, the perfect is sometimes used as a preterit (sense 2), and is then called the 'historical' perfect: thus, *scripsit ut rescriberēs; Miltiadēs est accūsātus; Dieu a créé le monde; er ist gestern angekommen.* The

English, and often the French, tense-phrases for the historical perfect differ from the preterit in expressing the past occurrences as recent (sense 5); thus, *he has taken his turn; je me suis levé à six heures.* Greek and Latin have a gnomic use of the perfect: *tulit pūnctum quī miscuit ūtile dulcī.*

v. The Pluperfect expresses the occurrence as finished at a past time (sense 2*c*); as, ἐγεγράφει, *scripserat, avait écrit.* Like the perfect, however, it is sometimes a 'point' tense. It then expresses simple occurrence prior to a given past time (sense 2); as in, *cum esset Dēmosthenes, ōrātōrēs clārī fuērunt, et anteā fuerant;* cf. *I heard* (sense 2) *before he had reported* (2*c*), with *I had heard* (1) *before he reported* (2). French has a distinct tense-phrase, the Past Anterior, for this latter sense; as, *quand il fut trouvé, il eut écrit.*

vi. The Future Perfect expresses the occurrence as finished at a given time to come (sense 9*c*); as in, *dūm tu haec legēs, ego illum fortasse convēnerō.* As a 'point' tense it may express sense 8. In Greek and Latin it sometimes expresses simple futurity (sense 9), which in Greek may be implied as immediate (sense 7); as, φράζε καὶ πεπράξεται, 'speak, and it shall at once be done.'

vii. The French Conditional is often a modal future implying contingency; as in, *elle n'oserait revenir.* By origin, however, it is a Future in the Past (sense 4): thus *écrirait = écrire + avait* (just as *écrira = écrire + a*); and as such it still expresses what is future relatively to a past time spoken of; as in, *je prévis qu'il écrirait.* The German subjunctive forms, *würde schreiben*, etc., answering to the old imperfect, *wurde schreiben*, fill the same rôle, as do English *should* and *would: he said he should* (was going to) *write.*

The tense-distinctions expressed by the inflected forms just named, together with others in the scheme given above, may be expressed by tense-phrases—"periphrastic tenses." Thus instead of πεποίηκε, 'he has done,' we may have πεποιηκώς ἐστιν ; for πράξει, *faciet*, we may have μέλλει πράττειν, *facturus est;* and we may improvise *will be going to write* for action impending in the future (sense 10); *would have written, aurait écrit*, for a 'future perfect in the past' (sense 4*c*), etc. English, with but two inflectional tenses, is rich in these periphrastic tenses.

The merely relative force of tense-forms becomes marked when they refer to standpoints in time spoken of. In εἶπεν ὅτι γενήσεται, 'he said that it *would happen*,' the happening expressed as future may be actually past, for the context gives this future a sort of modal setting as simply matter of report. Inflected speech has distinct modal forms for the tenses: as, γενήσοιτο, which in the example above would specify the happening as future only from the standpoint of εἶπεν. Certain tense-forms in these dependent constructions lose their distinction of the *time at* which their action occurs, and differ only in expressing its durative aspects. Thus in ἐὰν ποιῇ, ἐὰν ποιήσῃ, the present marks as progressive—'if he be doing' —what the aorist marks as simply occurring—'if he do'—both expressing the same *time* of occurrence.

This subordinating of tense to mood issues in the important principle of the "sequence of tenses," by which the tense in a dependent clause "follows," or is adjusted to, that in the main clause. In a "primary sequence" a tense expressing present or future time is followed by a like tense in the dependent clause; in a "secondary sequence" a tense expressing past time is followed by a like tense. Thus in, *he had no idea what twice two was, scrīpsit ut nōs monēret*, the past tenses *was, monēret*, express not past time, but simply a kind of concord between the verbs, by which the complex sentence is felt as a firmer unit. In most cases, to be sure, dependent past tenses which (like *monēret* here) carry an actually forward reference, take it from a context expressing purpose, anticipation, wish, possibility, etc. Their "sequence," therefore, is not merely mechanical, for they really have in view what *is to be* and what *was to be;* as in, *metuō ne absim; he meant to do so, if he were asked.* The perfect tenses (present and past, including the Greek aorist) here mark the action in prospect as a completed one: *dēmōnstrāvit, sī vēnissent, multōs interitūros.*

Where the context would make a tense-form refer forward from a past standpoint, it is apt to take on modal force. In '*Is he coming?*' '*Well, he was coming,*' *was* has shifted from marking the coming as formerly in prospect to implying it as of remoter likelihood now. Past tense in a thought-mood readily conveys this remoteness of present expectation: *wenn er doch endlich eine Wohnung fände, die ihm gefiele!*[1] It will be further displayed in clauses of supposition (p. 181).

(4) Number and Person. The distinction of form in a verb by which its assertion is marked as applying to one individual, or to more than one (in Greek, also to two), is hardly notional. '*He is just*' and '*they are just*' do not express a quantitative difference in 'being just.' Even between '*he runs*' and '*they run*,' though one might understand a difference in the number of acts of running, its expression in the verbs is superfluous, since it follows from the distinction between their subjects, *he* and *they*. Agreement in number between verb and subject is simply a grammatical concord marking the fact of their relationship.[2] The same is true of agreement in person. In '*I am content, if he is*,' *am* and *is* show formally their different reference to *I* and *he*. The latter alone express a real difference of "person," or of relationship to the discourse.

[1] *Report of the Joint Committee on Grammatical Terminology* (E. A. Sonnenschein, Chairman), pp. 35, 36 (1910).

[2] In Greek, nominatives in the neuter plural commonly take singular verbs; as in, τὰ οἰκήματα ἔπεσεν, 'the houses fell'; πάντα ῥεῖ.

The Modifiers: Adjective and Adverb. Examples of typical simple assertions will show what kinds of modifier are called for to phrase a subject and predicate, when we have "propositional names" for these terms:—

The bird calls.

Charles is { *angry.* / *king.* }

They { *seemed* { *tattered.* / *scarecrows.* } / *made Charles* { *angry.* / *king.* } }

Here the subject is in each case a noun or noun-equivalent. The predicate is either a notional verb—*calls*—or a copula (pure or semi-notional) +complement. The complement, again, is either a noun—*king, scarecrow*—or an attribute-word of other than subject habit—*angry, tattered.* Modifiers of a simple subject and predicate must therefore attach either (1) to nouns; or (2) to verbs and other attribute-words of non-subject habit. The former are Attributive modifiers; as, *white bird, bold Charles, true king, dingy scarecrows;* the latter are Adverbial modifiers; as, *calls angrily, calls the flock, very angry, tattered at elbows.* In *Charles is a true king*, the attributive develops the noun-idea *king;* in *Charles is truly king*, the adverbial *truly* attaches not to *king* but to *is*, making the predicate assert that 'his being king is true.'

The distinction of these terms is more convenient than scientific. Within the actual sentence-thought a phrasally expressed concept does not split into modified and modifying ideas. When one says, *black clouds gather fast; the nesting bird calls its mate*, one has no concern with broader assertions, *clouds gather*, *the bird calls*, which give the "head-words" of which grammar views *black*, *fast*, *nesting*, *mate* as the modifiers, narrowing down generic kernel-sentences to the given specific ones. Such a view reflects an interest, not in the *process* of speech, but in the economies *conditioning* speech. The further division of modifiers into attributive and adverbial, resting as it does on one between subject and predicate "habit" in the head-words, admits of doubtful border-cases, but it gives two broad categories of function to which words show certain answering features of habit and form.

As regards characteristic function, adjective and adverb are respectively attributive and adverbial; but, like the other parts of speech, they are constituted partly by content and form. The adjective is an attribute-word with a form or forms characteristic of attributive habit; δίκαιος 'just' (cf. δίκη, 'justice'); *formōsus*, *beautiful* (cf. *forma*, *beauty*). For subject-function it must take some special mark, as of position or with particles: '*the just* shall live by faith.' The adverb is an attribute-word with a characteristic form for adverbial habit; as, σποράδην, *scattered-ly* (cf. the adjective σποραδικός); *aliter*, *other-wise* (cf. *alius*, *other*).

i. ADJECTIVE. As to function, adjectives are either attributives—'*angry* Charles,' '*tattered* scarecrows'—or predicate complements—'is *angry*,' 'made (Charles) *angry*,' 'seemed *tattered*.' As to content, adjectives fall into two classes: (1) that of attribute notions of quality, property, and relationship—'proper' and 'descriptive' adjectives—as, *Turkish*, *Shakespearean; brave*, *dusty*, *great*, *loud*, *rapid;* (2) that of general limiting notions—'quantitative,' 'demonstrative,' 'distributive' adjectives—as, *much*, *half*, *some*, *two*, *second*, *twofold; this*, *such*, *other; each*, *every*, *either*. The slight intension of these limiting adjectives, together with their marked ordering and relating value in the context, bring them within the class of pronominal words (p. 101). As to form, adjectives of the languages here under view are apt to bear attributive suffixes: πολεμ-ικός, τλή-μων, *host-īlis*, *mont-anus*, *change-ful*, *care-less*, *picturesque*. In inflectional speech they show concord or agreement with their nouns in gender, number, and case; as in, *clārus imperātor*, *stellae lūcidae; gutes Kind.*[1] Neither of these threefold sets of formal variations carry any notional distinctions for adjectives. Concord between adjective and noun, therefore, is simply a grammatical device

[1] German 'descriptive' adjectives are not inflected when used predicatively; as in, *die Knaben sind gross*.

to mark the fact that these words join to express a complex concept. On the other hand, inflection for 'comparison'—as in *prior, primus; greater, greatest*—distinguishing the degree of the quality or relation expressed, is primarily notional, and figures in syntax only indirectly.

Attributive and predicative uses of the adjective can be distinguished in some languages by its position; as, ὁ σοφὸς ἀνήρ, 'the *wise* man,' but ὁ ἀνὴρ σοφός, 'the man *is wise*.' French differs from English in having the attributive adjective normally follow its noun; as, *un cheval noir.*[1] The expressive values of the French and English attributive positions are thus compared by Herbert Spencer:—

"If *a horse black* be the arrangement, immediately on the utterance of the word *horse*, there arises, or tends to arise, in the mind, a picture answering to that word; and as there has been nothing to indicate what kind of horse, any image of a horse suggests itself. Very likely, however, the image will be that of a brown horse, brown horses being the most familiar. The result is that when the word *black* is added a check is given to the process of thought. . . . But if, on the

[1] A few of the commonest, however,—*bon, grand, vieux, beau*, etc.,—are exceptions. English cardinal numerals used as ordinals—'chapter *three*' (third chapter), 'the year *eighty*'—and adjectives in a few such phrases as *the body politic, heirs male*, follow their nouns,—perhaps by French influence.

other hand, *a black horse* be the expression used, no such mistake can be made. The word *black* indicating an abstract quality, arouses no definite idea. It simply prepares the mind for conceiving some object of that colour, and the attention is kept suspended until that object is known. If, then, by the precedence of the adjective, the idea is conveyed without liability to error, whereas the precedence of the substantive is apt to produce a misconception, it follows that the one gives the mind less trouble than the other, and is therefore more forcible."[1]

To this it may be fairly objected that by itself *horse* is just as "abstract" as *black*, and does not imply brown colour or any other differencing feature. Words are not pressed for full implications the moment they fall on the ear, for one expects them to take some definition within the context. The advantage here claimed for the English order therefore can hardly be proved valid. English itself discards it in the case of phrased adjective equivalents—*a horse of bronze, horses for hire*—which follow their nouns.

ii. ADVERB. The content of a typical adverb is some element of a complex attribute; as, *illūc*, *thither; semper, always;* '*celeriter* currere,' 'to run *swiftly*,' '*very* loud.'[2] Its function in developing

[1] *The Philosophy of Style* (New York, 1888), pp. 12, 13.

[2] "An adverb is simply the attribute of an attribute; it bears the same relation to an attribute-word that an adjective does to a thing-word." H. Sweet: *Words, Logic, and Grammar* (Philolog. Soc. Trans., 1875–6, p. 489).

a predicate (explicit or conceptual) often calls for a distinction of form, since it involves the different application already noted (pp. 110, 141) between '*truly* king' and '*true* king,' 'stand *firmly*' and 'stand *firm*.' Inflected speech, therefore, has suffixes to form adverbs answering to most of the descriptive adjectives; as in, *prudent-er, prudent-ly;* and carries a distinction between their forms in comparison; as, *audācius*, 'boldlier:' cf. *audācior*, 'bolder.' English, however, has many so-called 'flat' adverbs, not differing in form from the adjectives; as in, 'run fast,' 'pay dear.'[1] No inflectional concord is made for adverbs.

iii. ATTRIBUTIVE AND ADVERBIAL NOUNS. Since the distinction of noun does not coincide with that of subject-word, we have to deal with noun-forms appearing as 'conceptual predicates'—that is, as attributive and adverbial modifiers. Thus, answering to a predicated class or defining thing—*ego patrōnus exstitī, Alfred was king, steel is a metal*—we may have an attributive noun ('appositive'); as, *Cicero patrōnus, Alfred king of England* or *King Alfred, the metal steel.* English, though having derivative suffixes to form adjectives from nouns, such as *autumn-al, gold-en, angel-ic*, tends in modern usage to express certain adjective senses by the bare, attributively-placed

[1] Some of these—as, *exceeding, wonderful*—are now archaic: *able to do exceeding abundantly; death grinned horrible a ghastly smile.*

noun; as in, 'the *autumn* meet,' 'a *gold* chain,' 'her *angel* face.' The attributive meaning here expressed is sufficiently evident from the meaning of both nouns in the phrase. It is one of quality when the attributive is taken as naming a *kind* of thing—distinction of kind resting on dominant quality; as, *boy orator, gentleman usher, moss rose, meat pie, loaf sugar.* It is one of relation when the attributive is taken as naming what the other thing *is for*, or *has to do with;* as *clothes brush, fire alarm, box factory, emergency ward.* Attributive nouns may carry the main sense of their phrases when the modified nouns, like the Chinese "classifiers," are of very general import: as in, *êrh*[4] *t'iao*[2] *yü*[2], 'two fish,' where *t'iao*[2] (literally 'branch,' 'twig') has faded into a mere notion of units or items. Cf. the pidgin-English *one piece man* (for *i*[1] *kê*[1] *jen*[2]); and English, *a dozen head of cattle.*

In inflected speech nouns take 'oblique' cases to express attributively or adverbially various relations to the things they denote. These really serve to keep a noun's content-notion at least indirectly named, while changing its grammatical function. Indo-European languages have as oblique cases, the genitive, dative, accusative, ablative, instrumental, and locative. Over against these cases stand the nominative for noun-function, and the vocative as a kind of noun-imperative. In the older view of language, each case was thought to have started with a root-notion, whether a grammatical one—subject, attributive, object—or a localising one, making the oblique cases answer to the questions, whence? where? whither? Such a view does not meet the evidence (see pp. 77–82) that the inflectional schemes in Greek and Latin were not developed from starting-points of single abstract meanings, but sifted down from an earlier profusion of concrete and diverse ones. Their resulting forms must be explained on grounds that are psychological rather than logical. For example, it is logically anomalous that nominative and accusative, the cases of subject and object, should in neuter nouns be alike: δῶρον, *templum*. But since action proceeds for the most part from animate beings to things, it is natural that the neuter, as the formal category for things, should have been early felt as an object-category, and that masculine and feminine words took its forms (λόγον, νῆσον, *puerum*) when the object-construction fell to them. That case-forms, again, are less discriminated in plurals (cf. nom., acc. *rēgēs*, *carmina;* dat., abl. *rēgibus*, *puerīs*) is doubtless because the many are not, like single things, sharply perceived in a set of relationships.[1]

The view of cases that takes each as proceeding from one broad meaning supplanted the older notion of cases that made their choice a matter of "governing" force in the verbs or prepositions

[1] Wundt: *Völkerpsychologie*, vol. i., pt. ii., pp. 65–68.

they occur with. Of the two views, however, the older seems nearer right in so far as it looks for case-meaning in the context. No case can have its uses brought under one general meaning. When, for example, a "general definition of the accusative" is offered in such a statement as that "it designates any kind of relation between noun and verb except that of subject to predicate,"[1] we must realise that any given relation expressed therewith gets specified otherwise than by the case. This is not to say that cases may not have specific primitive uses from which further uses have developed. But the derived uses do not stand to the primitive as special meanings within a general one. They are rather extensions, first of the early uses to uses felt as like, and then of these to still others. Thus, given the accusative in expressions where it marks that towards which there is motion—*hac iter Elysium*—and it will be applied where the goal is not spatial but something purposed—*venērunt questum*, 'they came to complain.' The notion of 'towards' passes easily into that of 'to'—*suās domōs abīre attigī metam*—where the accusative becomes associated with a "transitive force" in the verb. The resulting "direct object" construction naturally admits accusatives in which the notion 'to' is quite effaced: thus we get not only *sequī honorēs* but *fugere honorēs*. Accusatives may then show both direc-

[1] H. Paul: *Prinzipien der Sprachgeschichte*, p. 153.

tion and direct object for the same verb—*Catilīna juventūtem facinora ēdocēbat* (i.e. 'taught them bad ways'),—a construction which, once fixed as a formula, admits of being taken in reverse with the passive: *ēdoctus litterās.* Meanwhile, since relations of time are imaged in terms of space, the notion 'to' appears in expressions of duration—*annum tertium regnat*—even where the sense comes pretty roundabout: *puer decem annōs nātus.* Whether or not accusative uses actually developed by these steps,[1] this is the way usage spreads in the field of syntax. The logic of speech passes not by deduction from general meaning to particular application, but by analogy from particular to particular. Case-schemes, therefore, result not from the scope of categories, but from immediate similarities of sound and sense. These work in the main towards uniformity. Where the Greek used a "partitive" genitive with verbs meaning eat, drink, taste, touch, hear, desire, etc., and a dative with ἕπομαι, 'I attach myself,' the answering Latin expressions are all "levelled" to the accusative; and in the Latin ablative three older cases are merged.

Certain cases answer with some distinctness to relations of space. Thus we have not only a locative case, but in some languages a 'prosecutive' for that *moved along*, an 'illative' for that *moved*

[1] M. Bréal so understands it. See his *Semantics*, pp. 221–227, from which some examples above have been taken.

into, and an 'inessive' for that *having within*. But since things happen at once in space and time and as conditions, these relations are bound to blend in case-constructions. The relation 'from,' for example, holds not only for extent covered, but for time elapsed and for source or cause, the relation 'to' holds for extent to be covered, for time *until*, and for a *purposed* end. And when as in Greek, these uses are given a variety of nuances by prepositions, they become hard to classify at all. Wundt tries to make out "cases of inner determination," the nominative, genitive, accusative, and dative of indirect object, in which the relation expressed follows from the meaning of the words and need not be expressed by case-suffixes, and "cases of outer determination," in which the relation must be made explicit by suffixes or particles. The distinction obliges him to look for over-subtle differences of sense (for example, between *Romam ire* and *nach Rom gehen*), and seems to be rather artificially superposed upon the facts. Apart from given particular instances we cannot say what relations will follow from stem-meanings, and what will not; and when we review the whole range of instances we cannot find any formal scheme answering to the relations so classed actually carried out.[1]

[1] Wundt's distinction here (*Logik*, i., p. 138; *Völkerpsychologie*, I., ii., p. 83 ff.) is criticised both by Sütterlin (*op. cit.*, p. 103 ff.) and Paul (*op. cit.*, 4th. ed., p. 152).

i. The Genitive,[1] expressing certain limiting and defining relations between nouns, is often called the 'adjective case.' With the possessive sense, 'belonging or pertaining to,' it is, like an adjective, either attributive or predicative; as in, *Plato's doctrine* (cf. *the Platonic doctrine*), *this doctrine is Plato's.* The limiting uses of the genitive are even more adjective-like; as in, *a moment's delay, to-day's news* (cf. *a momentary delay, die heutigen Nachrichten*). So are descriptive genitives, expressing material or quality; as in, κρήνη ἡδέος ὕδατος, 'a spring of fresh water;' *flūmina lactis, vir summae probitātis.* The 'partitive' genitive, expressing a divided whole—as in, *plāna urbis*, 'the level parts of the town'—and the 'objective' genitive—*precātiō deōrum*, '*for sin's rebuke and my Creator's praise*'—can perhaps be taken as extensions of the possessive, but further genitive uses point to origins widely diverse. A case which, as in *amor patris*, marks either subject or object, can not be described except by giving it the equally vague synonym *of.* It simply marks attributive nouns, expressing almost any relation with which they may enter into complex concepts. As Pro-

[1] Lat. *genetivus*, a mistranslation of γενική, the case "of the genus." In older English the genitive was an adverbial case as well: *love ne lordshipe wol noght, hir thankes* [willingly], *have no felaweshipe.* The loss of this use for the suffix has left a number of genitives—*needs, sideways, sometimes*—as unrelated adverbs, though certain genitive phrases retain it: *of a truth, of course; he would come of an evening.* Cf. *geht eures Weges*, 'go your ways.'

fessor Morris remarks,[1] the relation expressed in *pars militum, aliquid bonī, pondus aurī, nomen amicitiae, ira deōrum*, is chiefly a question of the meaning of the words. In English, the genitive (which is the sole inflected case remaining in nouns) has tended to become limited to the possessive or closely analogous senses, and thus to be restricted to names of persons.[2] On the other hand, the English genitive suffix has become free to attach to a whole phrase, like an independent relating particle; as in, *the King of Prussia's decree, somebody else's sister.*[3]

ii. The Dative has characteristic adverbial uses, in which the relation expressed answers broadly to the senses of *to* and *for*. The first use expresses the 'indirect object,' viz., that which takes part in an action or more or less actively receives it, as distinguished from the 'direct object,' which is either produced by the action, or more or less passively acted upon. "Thus in *dedit puerō librum*, 'he gave the boy a book,' or *fēcit mihi iniūriam*, 'he did me a wrong,' there is an idea of

[1] *Principles and Methods in Latin Syntax*, p. 84.

[2] Except in certain stereotyped phrases—*a summer's day, a week's wages, a stone's throw, a hand's breadth*, etc.—it suggests in names of things a personification; as in the 'objective' sense quoted above, in the 'appositional' genitive (*Britain's isle*), and in, *a mountain's base, the ages' flight*, etc.

[3] The opposite to this freedom of position is shown in "parasynthetic" compounds by the participle suffix, which keeps to its verb-stem, even when applying to elements that follow. Thus *uncared-for* is not *un-* + *cared* + *for* but *un-* + (*care for*) + *-ed*.

the boy's receiving the book, and of my feeling the wrong. Hence expressions denoting persons, or things with personal attributes, are more likely to be in the dative than those denoting mere things."[1] The second use is the 'dative of interest,' indicating that which an action serves. Thus *laudat mihi patrem* implies a regard for me as its purpose, which would not appear in *laudat patrem meum.* A like notion of regard shows more vaguely in the familiar 'ethical dative:' "Villain, I say, knock *me* at this gate;" "A terrible demon of a woman . . . claps *you* an iron cap on her head."

iii. The Accusative[2] is the case of the direct object. It completes the meaning of a verb, either (1) in a 'cognate' object making explicit what is already implied in the verb; as in, *he had bled so mychel blood;* (2) in a 'factitive' object, expressing what the act results in; as in, πρεσβεύουσι τὴν εἰρήνην, 'they make peace;' cf. *to drill a hole, to paint pictures;* (3) in the more external object of verbs in the common transitive uses; as in, *Brūtus Caesarem interfēcit.* The accusative is thus an adjunct to verbs, extending as such to adverbial expressions other than object-words, especially to those of time and place; as in, ἔμεινε τρεῖς ἡμέρας, 'he remained three days;' *domum iit*, 'he went home.'

[1] Allen and Greenough: *New Latin Grammar*, p. 224.

[2] This rather absurd name is derived from a mistranslation of αἰτιατική, by which the Greeks discussed it as the *causal* case.

iv. The Ablative proper expresses the relation *from.* It is thus used in expressing (1) separation, as in the formula of banishment: *eī aquā et īgnī interdīcitur;* (2) source, as in, *quō sanguine crētus;* and such senses of cause and comparison as arise in the notions of separation and source: *ars ūtilitāte laudātur; lacrimā nihil citius ārēscit*—the ablative here marking that from which one reckons in comparing.

v. The Instrumental, expressing *with* or *by,* and the Locative, expressing *at, in,* remain as distinct cases only in a few forms of Old English and Latin.

The conceivable relations between things are of course far too numerous to be distinguished precisely by these half-dozen cases. Case-constructions, therefore, owe whatever precision they have to what the words themselves imply. It is only the stem-meaning of a case-form that can give us a 'possessive' genitive, a dative 'of interest,' an ablative 'of time.' And whenever the construction is described by naming the kind of word upon which the case-form depends—as, the 'dative after verbs of pleasing, favouring, trusting,' the 'two accusatives after verbs of naming and calling,' the 'genitive after verbs of remembering,' etc.—its meaning is at least partly a matter of context.[1] Furthermore, so long as the specific relation is thus made clear, it hardly matters which

[1] E. P. Morris: *op. cit.*, p. 85.

of the larger categories of relation one views it as deriving from. Much the same relationships, therefore, are expressed now with one case, now with another. Thus cf. *patris similis esse*, 'to be his *father's* like,' with *sīmia quam similis nōbīs*, 'the ape, how like *to us!*' *vir summae virtūtis* with *mulier eximiā pulchritūdine*. Analogy, working among these vague case-meanings, seems to have followed the most haphazard associations. In some instances it has blurred their distinctions both in meaning and form. Thus the Latin locative is almost lost by its merging with the dative and ablative. The Greek ablative is wholly lost, its uses having been assimilated chiefly by the genitive. The instrumental became merged with the dative in Greek and Old English, with the ablative in Latin. Case-endings, therefore, were bound to fall short of expressive precision, even with the help of stem-meanings and context, so that as time went on their meanings came to be further specified by added particles, especially for relations of space.[1] These relating particles, originally adverbs, became the prepositions which in modern languages have made cases superfluous (see p. 70).

Instead of simple oblique cases, therefore, we

[1] In classical Latin a large variety of relations were still expressed by case-forms. In their literal uses these tended to take on prepositions, and in their figurative uses, to retain the bare case-constructions. Allen and Greenough: *New Latin Grammar*, p. 209.

may have as attributive and adverbial terms, "case-phrases" with prepositions. In inflected speech these phrases retain the oblique cases in their nouns; as in, *negōtiātor ex Āfricā; in Āfricam nāvigāvit.* With certain prepositions a difference of case here marks a distinction of sense. Thus, *mānsit in aedibus, das Buch liegt auf dem Tische,* express with ablative and dative the relation *where;* while *venit in aedīs, ich lege es auf den Tisch,* express with accusative the relation *whither.* Even here, however, the context alone would often carry this distinction. The case-endings, in fact, must lose their importance after prepositions, and tend to become either confused until one of them supplants the rest; or slurred in utterance until they are 'levelled' and finally lost. Thus in late Latin, as in vernacular modern Greek, the accusative became the ordinary case after all prepositions;[1] while in English nouns, all cases but the genitive are reduced to one neutral form. Most senses conveyed in the older oblique cases are therefore now carried by relating particles alone. Expressively the gain is twofold: (1) differences of declension made the older nouns show different forms in one and the same case (e.g., the Latin genitives, *rosae, puerī, arbōris, manūs*), where the

[1] The *Report of the Joint Committee on Grammatical Terminology* cites '*Saturninus cum suos discentes,*' from before A.D. 79. See Meyer-Lübke: *Grammaire Comparée des Langues Romanes*, ii., p. 29.

preposition (e.g., *of*) keeps but one form for the same sense; (2) one case covered loosely several senses which the prepositions distinguish: thus the general relation 'where' covered by the locative is now specified as *at*, *on*, or *in*. Such a distinction with both cases and prepositions as that just instanced for 'where' and 'whither' can be supplied simply with a new preposition—as *into*—when it is needed; thus, *he ran first into the yard and then in it.* The sole English noun-phrases showing both case-form and preposition are the so-called 'double possessives,' which often make a useful difference of sense. Thus, *father's picture* may mean either 'a picture *of father*' or a picture *of father's*.

A desire to keep in view "the likeness of English, so far as it extends, to the more highly inflected languages" has led the British Joint Committee on Grammatical Terminology to advise the use of Latin case-names in describing English noun-constructions.[1] Common names, however, are here apt to suggest more points of likeness than really exist. There can be no harm in calling *to London*, *with me*, "case-phrases," but "dative" and "accusative" are too vague as sense-categories to apply profitably when their case-suffixes are lacking. The "positional" dative distinguished as preceding a noun-accusative cannot be told apart from constructions with two

[1] *Report* (1910), p. 25.

accusatives. Thus, as Professor Jespersen remarks,[1] in *I told the boy stories, asked the boy questions, heard the boy his lessons, took the boy long walks, kissed him good-night, called him a rascal, tied him hand and foot*, it is arbitrary to say where dative goes out and accusative comes in. Two object-words with a verb seem, in fact, to take the disposal that throws the one felt as more prominent—whether dative or accusative—to the end. Thus, *I taught the boys Latin; tell him this; we 'll show it you; bring the book to me.*

A question remains whether or not there survives a linguistic feeling for a case, where the case-form itself is lost. M. Bréal understands the objection to using an unrepeated *vous* in, *il sait que je vous ai toujours respecté et porté une vive affection* to lie in the fact that an idea of the lost dative lingers in the mind, partly as a linguistic tradition, partly by a reminiscence of—*je le respecte et l u i porte*, etc.[2] The same survival has been claimed for English, where a word must be repeated as in, *a question which arose, and which they long discussed.*[3] In such examples, however, the repetition is called for by the change of logical relation—subject, direct object, indirect object—in which the repeated words appear. But differ-

[1] 'History of the English Language in its Relation to Other Subjects' (*Englische Studien*, vol. xxxv, 1905) p. 9.

[2] *Semantics*, pp. 50, 51.

[3] See C. T. Onions: *Advanced English Syntax*, p. 87.

ences of logical relation are far from coinciding regularly with differences of case. A linguistic feeling for the latter can safely be alleged, only where such necessarily repeated words correspond to older case-distinctions, but make little or no logical difference. It is doubtful whether instances of this kind exist. No objection would be raised to *attendre et servir le roi,* although the older language would require a change to the dative: *rēgem exspectāre et eī servīre.* Certain prepositional phrases, however, in which the preposition seems not called-for logically, may reflect an older dative or genitive: *il plaît à tout le monde* (cf. *placet omnibus*); *near to the fire* (cf. *nēah pæm fȳre*); *think of an idea; smell of a flower.*

Verbal Nouns and Adjectives. Since noun, adjective, and verb make word-categories only by a concurrence of features, notional words must, in thought of any complexity, show hybrid forms: verb-nouns and verb-adjectives. Such words, taking noun and adjective constructions while keeping a verb regimen of subject, object, etc., are brought increasingly into play in the more developed speech of people capable of some abstractness in thinking. At their simplest (*dolēre malum est; learn to labour; jangling bells*) they show little notional difference from other nouns and adjectives of action, and seem even superfluous, for our languages do not lack affixes for making such nouns and adjectives from verb-stems: *vocā-tiō, mōlī-tiō, resist-ance, embezzle-ment; pugn-ax, bib-ulus, tire-some, correct-ive.* These derivatives, however, serve another end from that of verbals, and crystallise the verb-notion in ways reflecting a different angle of view; viz.—

i. A derivative affix takes the verb-notion more absolutely, with its act or process viewed apart from any setting, whereas the verbal affix takes it as proceeding from an agent, bearing on a recipient, occurring in present, past, or future, sometimes even as obligatory: that is, with its aspects of voice, tense, and even mood. Thus a noun in *-ation* makes no point of voice-distinction: *our preparation for war* may according to context mean either 'our preparing' or 'our being prepared.'

ii. A derivative affix restricts its application to those verb-senses that are in some special demand, while the verbal affix, like an inflection, applies throughout. Thus of the two meanings of *preach*—'discourse publicly on a religious topic' and 'sermonise; give moral advice officiously'—only the second appears in *preachment,* whereas *preaching* takes over both senses, even in their transitive use: *his preaching repentance.*

iii. Derivative nouns run to transferred senses denoting no longer the acts or processes themselves, but what is causally associated with them; as in, *to find nutriment; caught in wire entanglements.*

Give me *t o k n o w* *Thee,* asks for an experience, where *give me* *k n o w l e d g e* *of Thee* would ask for its result. Derivative adjectives take some specialisation with the affix. Thus *pugn-ax, aud-ax; correct-ive, act-ive* mean not simply 'fighting,' 'correcting,' etc., but *tending to* fight, correct, etc.

The characteristic use of a verbal, as in *their launching the ship promptly,* takes from its likeness to the formula of assertion (*they launch the ship promptly*) a vividness that is lacking to plain noun and adjective constructions (*the prompt launching of the ship*).[1] By its means a complex sentence admits more precise inner adjustments of sense-relation, while keeping its organic form as a judgment-group transparent: *our enemy's deploying eastward showed them to be moving camp.*

As nouns and adjectives the verbals may stand as subject, predicate, attributive, direct-object, or in the adverbial relation expressed by an oblique case. As verbs they have a "kernel" meaning of action or occurrence; they may carry the distinctions of voice, mood, and tense, usually shown by formatives; and they may take a verb-regimen with subject, object, adverb, or complement (predicative adjective or noun). One can describe them conveniently, therefore, by help of a diagram showing these two sets of features in columns that cross. Where a feature is *formally* marked (by

[1] *He thought of betting heavily* suggests the act in view as more concretely his than would *he thought of heavy betting.*

article, preposition, or affix) its symbol may be given in black-faced type. Thus English verbals in *-ing* make constructions as follows:—

VERB. / NOUN–ADJ.		Content a	Voice b	Mood c	Tense d	Regimen e
Subject	1	×				×
Predicative	2	×	×			
Attributive	3	×				
Direct Obj.	4	×	×		×	
Adverbial	5	×				×

1ae. *His chanting the words aloud gave pleasure;* cf. *the loud chanting of the words* (1a). Older English used also a third construction, *the* + verbal + object: *in the delaying death; the locking up the spirits.*

2ab. *The new church is building.* Originally an adverbial case-phrase, *a-build-ing* for *on* (or *in*) *building* (5a). The verbal is here passive (cf. also *the bread is baking; lunch is getting ready*); but in *I go hunting*, etc., it is active.

3a. *a danc'ing master; danc'ing child'ren.* Stress here distinguishes two sorts of meaning for the attributive.[1]

[1] The Old English verbal adjective in *-ende* became assimilated to the abstract noun in *-inge* (earlier *-ung*), which later took on a verbal regimen. Their attributive meanings, however, are still distinct, the former giving an attribute; the latter a defining relation: thus *drink'ing water* is not 'water that drinks' (cf. *a drink'ing man'*), but 'water for drinking.'

4abd. *He mentioned its having been written.*
The whole phrase is taken as a perfect passive of *writing* answering to the Greek γεγράφθαι.

5ae. *We stop you from speaking rashly.*
In English such verbal case-phrases are now formed only in *-ing*, where they could once be formed with the 'infinitive:' *what went ye out for to see; could save the son of Thetis from to die* (cf. *sans lui parler; ohne zu schreiben*).

These examples show how the traditional way of describing verbals is complicated. Their names —infinitive, gerund, supine, participle—apply to types of form, which indeed distinguish ways of taking the verb-meaning, but ways that cannot be paralleled throughout by the corresponding forms in other languages. Greek, for example, has a set of infinitive forms for past, present, and future both active and passive, which with the article can take all the constructions of a verbal noun. Latin divides these constructions between three sets of forms—infinitive, gerund, supine—supplying a future infinitive from the participle: *spērat diū sē vīctūrum* (3 ade); English has for some of them two sets of forms, and German one, all but the present being phrasal; as, *having written, to have been written, geschreiben worden sein.* But the Greek infinitive makes no constructions like *it is to seek* (2abd), *they were to have come* (2ad); *er blieb stehen* (2a); *wir ritten spazieren* (5a), *er hat*

Wein im Keller liegen (5ae). The Latin future passive participle is not simply future, like γραφησόμενος, but takes the modal colouring for which Greek has a distinct form: *epistula scribenda est;* ἐπιστόλη γραπτέα ἐστίν (2abc); cf. *eine zu stürmende Festung* (3abc); and the English verb-noun in *-ing* has no difference of form from the participle. It seems misleading, therefore, to name modern verbals by their partial analogies to Greek and Latin. Nothing is gained by descrying first an infinitive in *this is misdoing* after τοῦτό ἐστι τὸ ἀδικεῖν (1a), then a gerund in *cause for taking arms* after *causa arma capiendī* (3ae), and a participle in *scouts report the enemy moving;* nor, again, an infinitive in *I shall dare to die* (τλήσομαι τό κατθανεῖν), and a supine in *they came to complain of wrongs* (*vēnērunt questum iniūriās*). Nor should translation be allowed to blur one's sense for idiosyncrasies in the way two mediums dispose the thought. *He came to ransom his daughter* (5ae) is not precisely ἦλθε λυσόμενος θύγατρα (2abde); *he is ashamed to say this* appears with differences in αἰσχύνεται τοῦτο λέγων and αἰσχύνεται τοῦτο λέγειν; and *I heard German spoken* gives a passive turn to *ich hörte Deutsch sprechen* (4ae). It is especially misleading to parse these phrases in terms that emphasise the noun as their special point of remark,—as the word "governed" by verb and preposition and "modified" by the adjective term. Such is not a true account of ἤκουσε

Κῦρον ἐν Κιλικίᾳ ὄντᾳ; *dat operam agrīs colendīs; ā conditā urbe; 't was at the royal feast for Persia won*:—phrases in which the noun-verbal complex pivots upon its latter element. Where the meaning is brought about less by a compounding of several word-meanings than by a sort of carom between them, any word-by-word parsing describes the parts only by misconstruing the whole.

VII. THE SENTENCE-WHOLE

The Sentence in Thought and Expression. Since grammatical study makes its special field the sentence, it gets little flattery from the fact that authorities still disagree as to what a sentence is. Paul defines it as "the linguistic expression or symbol for the fact that two or more ideas unite in the mind of the speaker; and the medium for bringing about the same union of ideas in the mind of the hearer."[1] This definition serves to set aside the misconception that requires for the sentence a finite verb, and to cover all kinds of sentence, such, for example, as appear in *omnia praeclara rara; like master, like man; Träume, Schäume; this to me!* But against it Wundt objects that it presupposes ideas as first lying apart in the speaker's mind, to be then drawn together into sentence-units, whereas thinking actually proceeds by analysing ideal wholes into their idea-units. His own definition of the sentence as the expression of such a purposive analysis we have quoted on p. 47. That views so divergent can be held of the unit of discourse will not seem strange if we reflect:

[1] H. Paul: *op. cit.*, p. 121.

(1) that the sentence-thought comes differently to speaker and hearer, presenting itself to the former as a whole, and to the latter, piecemeal; (2) that its expression is partly conditioned by its context. As a thought the sentence is essentially an ideal content charged with purposive relevance to a notional context that its speaker is concerned with. Precisely *how* it is relevant is disclosed by a momentary analytic phase, bringing out conceptual factors through which the train of associations lead; but this analysis, by which the thought becomes shot through, as it were, with noun, adjective, and verb,[1] does not dissipate its impression as a unit, for the sentence-thought is itself a conceptual factor in a larger whole. Of these two aspects the analytic one is what interests the writer or speaker, for he begins with the whole and must show its factors, while the synthetic one seems more the concern of reader or hearer, who begins with the factors and must take in how they unite. Paul's definition evidently reflects the latter standpoint. But it misses the fact that ideas make up a sentence not merely by their sum, but by a value-relation with which their sum is charged.

So much may be true of the sentence in thought, and still leave a question as to what makes a sentence in words. In conversation, of course, words are helped out by looks, tone, gesture, so that

[1] W. James: *Pluralistic Universe*, Appendix A, p. 348.

sentences need be verbal only so far as their constituent ideas do not get expression otherwise. Indeed a sentence may always be short of words where its ideas are sufficiently evident from the context. The sentence-thought is here complete, but its expression is scant. What we then have is a word or phrase with the *value* of a sentence. Such words and phrases appear to be of three classes:—

i. PREDICATES. We have already remarked (p. 22) that an exclamation like *shame! how true! que de fleurs!* is really a predicate, having as subject what is simply accepted by speaker and hearer as present to mind. So also are imperatives (*look! tenez!*) and any words that answer a given "part-question" (see p. 182); thus, *who killed Cock Robin? I! When was Milton born? In 1806.* These answers, of course, do not make formal predicates, since they are offered to supply the subject and adverbial blanks, *who? when?* etc.; but they are what we shall distinguish (pp. 174–5) as the predicates in thought.

ii. FACT-WORDS. *Yes, no,* and their equivalents—*certainly, not at all,* etc.—presuppose the complete content of a sentence as given, but without its reference to fact—a reference which the sentence puts in question for them to supply. Thus, *has the bell rung?* offers a possible assertion. *Yes* or *no* closes the circuit that imparts to it real assertion.

iii. PARALLELS. Sentence-equivalents such as *much cry, little wool; borrow, sorrow; summum ius, summa iniuria; point d'argent, point de Suisse; heisse Bitte, kalter Dank*, seem different from other sentence-phrases in that their unexpressed parts need not be given in their context. In their character as proverbs, however, they assume a background of common experience that amounts to a permanent social context. *Much cry, little wool*, for example, points the bare antithetic parallel in a sentence that is ground-circuited, as it were, by the common knowledge of a story about shearing hogs.

Since any sense-complex sums within itself a whole series of judgments, the distinction between simple sentences, with but one explicit predicate, and compound sentences, is a somewhat external one. Where modifiers are expanded into clauses (*the sinful soul shall die; the soul that sinneth, it shall die*), the resulting "complex" sentence shows a stronger definition in its parts, rather than any added content. It is simply the fully expressed opposite of the "scant" sentence. The conventional practice of calling sentences "compound" only when made up of coördinate clauses, has some risk of misleading.[1]

Compound sentences take three types of formula:—

[1] The terms "double" and "multiple" are recommended for these cases by the British Joint Committee on Grammatical Terminology (*Report*, 1910, p. 12).

i. Parataxis: $s^\frown p + s'^\frown p'$, *the bell rang; I woke.* Here two simple sentences felt as jointly expressing a single thought are arranged as detached units side by side. This is doubtless the embryo form of the complex sentence. Arrangement side by side was enough to show the *fact* of a close relation between the two units, and primitive speakers did not trouble to show the *nature* of their relation by subordinating one to the other grammatically. We cannot say, however, that the subordination was not felt. The nature of relations that we now express with "dependent" clauses, was in simpler modes of thought not sharply discriminated: cause and effect, act and purpose, condition and conclusion, all being taken in as sequence in space and time.[1] But whenever of two sentences the second analyses or defines an element in the first (*here comes John; he is the one to tell us*), or briefly sums up what is analysed out in the first, or presents with the first the complementary parts of a parallel or contrast (*he must increase; I must decrease*), both speaker and hearer must, as part of their grasp of the train of thought, feel a difference between these relations. In actual talk such differences in parataxis get some expression from tempo, tone, and sentence-accent, so that we should not assume the primitive structure to have

[1] E. P. Morris: *op. cit.*, p. 213. For the ideas sketched in this paragraph I am much indebted to the chapter on Parataxis, pp. 113–149.

shown no more relating clues than appear in these written sequences. Our grammatical account here is apt to suffer from the fact that a long tradition of study confined to written speech has brought us unprepared to notice and describe the reflex features of utterance. When these are taken into account there is hardly such a thing as parataxis, defined strictly as "the arrangement side by side of *detached* sentence-units."

The old paratactic formula is perhaps still transparent in such sentences as, *ego ista studia nōn improbō, moderāta modo sint; ich behaupte, er ist ein Maler; ask me no questions, I 'll tell you no lies; he found a coat* | *that was torn; I heard that* | *you were sick; I know* | *who did it*, where *that* and *who* have weakened from demonstrative and interrogative into connectives. Traces of it occur in so-called "omitted relative" constructions, where the two members might be set off thus: (*there is* [*a devil*) *haunts thee*]; (*I tell you* [*news*) *will comfort you*]; (*he groneth as* [*a bore*) *lith in our stie*]. The correlated sentences are often marked as such in Old English by answering demonstratives: *se . . . se; þæt . . . þæt; þǣr þīn goldhord is, þǣr is þīn heorte.* The later subordination of one sentence then took place with a change from demonstrative to relative: *where thy treasure is, there will thy heart be also.* In this way a growing feeling for adjustments of emphasis that give the sentence-complex perspective brought into use fuller and preciser formulas with conjunctions. The resulting grammatical subordination or Hypotaxis, is of course further expressed by mood (*quaesō ut īgnōscās*), sometimes by verb-position (*Ludwig, der ein geschickter Maler war*). A variety of expressive features, including stress, intonation, and pause, take part even in such slight complexes as *er sprach, als wenn er reich wäre.*

In speaking of clauses as coördinate and subordinate, one must bear in mind that these terms do not apply here in their logical senses. The "orders" of value in members of a sentence-complex depend not on what they include, but on their felt prominence. A subordinate clause stands to its principal much as an upper partial to the ground tone in a musical note: its secondary status is only relative and for the nonce.

ii. Serial subjects and predicates: $(s+s')^\frown p$, *another love succeeds, another race;* $s^\frown(p+p')$, *dust thou art, to dust returnest;* $(s+s')^\frown(p+p')$, *Peter and Paul travelled and preached.* Subject, or predicate, or both, are here group-terms, so that the relation they assert develops what is felt as not so much a concept as a conceptual aggregate. Sentences can thus, without losing unity, run a whole series of associated ideas into either term, so long as they preserve between subject and predicate the same *kind* of expressed relation. They make an economy in the analytic movement involved, and reflect a larger grasp of ideas. Thus $s^\frown p + s^\frown p' + s'^\frown p + s'^\frown p'$ as four assertions carry the thought no further than $(s+s')\frown(p+p')$, in which it makes the analytic advance at one stroke. That a compound sentence of this pattern differs from a "complex" one only by the equal prominence felt between its associated ideas can be seen from the ease with which it turns complex, upon any change in their emphasis; as in, *Peter, like Paul, travelled that he might preach.*

iii. SENTENCE SUBJECTS AND PREDICATES: $\widehat{s\frown p}\,P$, *that I am old is true;* $S\,\widehat{s\frown p}$, *the trouble is you always grumble.* A subject or predicate term that is itself something asserted has a tang of concreteness that cannot be rendered by a phrasal term, as in, *the trouble is your habit of grumbling.* The same quality is had in the formula of *turn about is fair play*, but in *whom* [=*those whom*] *the gods love die young; they say I am old*, we pass to attributive and adverbial clauses. Even there, a vividness of effect seems at times to have prompted the use of a clause where the construction would naturally be phrasal; as in, *they made ready the present against Joseph came at noon.*

Since the thought in a sentence must take such shape in words as their syntactic "habit" makes them tractable to, its logical predicate, which the context shows to make the actual advance in thought, will at times lie elsewhere than in the formal one constituted by its verb. This happens freely in uttered sentences, where stress and intonation make the logical predicate stand out, however weakly it may be set in the grammatical formula. *Charles' came yesterday* really says that 'one who came yesterday was Charles.' Words, especially in analytic speech, are so imperfectly mobile as to resist a free displacement for expressive effect. But the speaking voice modulates with such nicety to the mental movement behind them that a sentence may show the bearing of its thought less by its grammatical than by its musical form.

Kinds of Sentence. In classifying sentences as statements, questions, exclamations, and commands, grammar has looked—with better success than in classifying words—to a single and essential ground. Such a ground lay inevitably in their meaning, for differences of meaning, after all, are what speech-forms intend, and what must be appealed to ultimately for sentence-distinctions that are to lead to anything. But in looking through speech to the informing thought one must discriminate what is actually *expressed* in sentences from what subattentively *fringes* them, or may be supplied in afterthought to *explain* them. One needs here whatever light our discussion thus far affords, to picture them in relation to the whole flow of mental life.

The stream of consciousness is continuous, not only between successive moments, but as taken in cross-section at any one moment. "No matter how small a tract of it be taken, it is always a much-at-once, and contains innumerable aspects and characters which conception can pick out, isolate, and thereafter always intend. It shows duration, intensity, complexity or simplicity, excitingness, pleasantness or their opposites. Data from all our senses enter it, merged in a general extensiveness of which each occupies a big or little share. Yet all these parts leave its unity unbroken,"[1] for they "compenetrate and diffuse into their neighbours in every direction." Consciousness, however, is no inert bubble-fountain: it is dominated by a selective concern for whatever furthers its own life. This is always centering upon one point and another within it, so that its flow is dotted through with emphases,—salient points felt as relevant to the immediate business of living. What we have called judgment is just such a focusing of attention upon this and that element of the continuum. But every element so emphasised takes part in the after-life of consciousness. It is thereby abstracted and remembered, and may take a name by which it is identified again. From a mere *that*, as James says, it becomes a *what*, an idea, leading the twofold existence that we began by observing in ideas: first, as an image recurring at will as a faintly perceptual item; second, as a fixed abstract meaning that interprets experience. In this their secondary nature, generalised out of

[1] W. James: "Percept and Concept" (in *Some Problems of Philosophy*, 1911), p. 49.

the perceptual instances, ideas are matter not of momentary being but of intent, and as such must be thought of platonically as static sense-patterns *above* the stream and simply mirrored in it by the mind's ordering activity. As reason matures, more and more of the perceptual flux becomes understood in the conceptual order. "Aspect within aspect, quality after quality, relation upon relation, absences and negations as well as present features, end by being noted and their names added to the store of nouns, verbs, adjectives, conjunctions, and prepositions by which the human mind interprets life."[1]

An uttered thought, therefore, expresses the conceptual bearings disclosed in any part of the conscious field by the focusing interest. Its unity results from the fact that attention absorbs only what is there relevant to that interest, and thereby prompts its concepts to verbalise into a conforming whole. Its word-sequence, then, does not mean that its concepts are drawn serially from the mental flow, for the thought "flashes *across* the mind;" but since a current of associations brings continually new parts of the flux under view, the sequence of thoughts must take place by a series of acts of attention, and discourse moves off by sentences, as walking by steps, in response to successive adjustments. The sentence-thought is therefore something to be valued in terms both

[1] W. James: *op. cit.*, p. 52.

of scope and of relevance—the former in its conceptual content, the latter in the speaker's interest. Content, it is now clear, can no more give the measure of a sentence than of a word. It will not even distinguish sentence from word, since the two may coincide for notions either complex, as in *cantavisset*, or simple, as in *Alas!* The differencing feature of the sentence is simply the energising interest to which its worded concepts conform. That interest may be practical, offering the concepts for present action to turn upon; or it may be theoretical, developing their relations by way of furthering knowledge. Differences in the kind of interest, therefore, give the ground for distinguishing types of sentence, and since sentences pass between a speaker and a hearer, it is easy to see that the four recognised types meet the varieties of concern that this relation presupposes. It will keep this fact in mind to begin our sketch of these types not with the most important, but with those in which this subjective aspect is vivid.

i. The EXCLAMATIVE sentence offers its content as matter of wonder, joy, indignation, or other emotion on the speaker's part. It may take the full predicative form, as in, *ut me mălus abstulit error! qu'il est riche! how true it is!* or it may be scant, as in, *welch eine Wendung durch Gottes Fügung! how true!* Its lower limit is the interjection, which in such instances as *Oh! Aha! Ouch! Whew!* passes below the level of speech altogether, for these outcries are not so much symbols that *mean* the feeling as mere symptoms betraying it. Exclamative sentences are formed by acts of judgment, and hence contain assertion: but they present it, so to speak, obversely, making their special issue the feeling that impels it.

ii. The IMPERATIVE sentence presents the speaker's will that what it says shall be acted on. Sentence-words of command include not only verb imperatives, as *come! beware!* but vocatives, as in *Rome, thou art shamed!* for the noun here addresses an appeal for attention. In the third person, where command must be indirect, it often weakens into wish, and gives border-cases between request and simple exclamation; as in, *ruin seize thee! may his tribe increase!*

iii. The ASSERTIVE sentence makes explicit a descriptive judgment. Since the speaker's attitude in asserting is simply that of imputing truth, it is more or less taken for granted, so that sentences of this type seem to offer their meaning more objectively than do those of exclamation and command. The two aspects of meaning that we have remarked in general names—their implication and their application—give two kinds of logical character to general assertions: one as abstract, another as concrete. Thus *trespassers will be prosecuted* means, when taken concretely, that 'certain trespassers are to get an incurred prosecution;' when taken abstractly, that 'trespassing incurs prosecution.' Subject and predicate here stand either as: (1) *there are S's and all of them are P;* or (2) *if S, then P.* That is, assertions of the type *all S are P* are either Categorical, describing experienced fact; or Hypothetical, describing the nature of cases. In many contexts it is indifferent which of these characters is understood, and apart from some context they cannot be distinguished at all.

The abstract character of hypothetical assertion is made explicit in the Conditional form: *if A is B, then it is C.*[1] Here one should avoid the common mistake of saying that the sentence "asserts the consequence of a supposition," for this would identify the sentence with its consequent clause. What the whole sentence asserts is a relation between two clausal terms, viz., that one is asserted on condition of the other's being true. This relation—*if S, then P*—describes the *nature* of S without affirming its *existence.* By its formal intention, therefore, the sentence stresses implication rather than application, and is abstract.

The distinction of abstract and concrete, however, rests so unstably upon theoretical or practical interest, that even a sentence with condition is

[1] This form is logically the typical one. *If A, then B* (if carbon, then inflammable) merely abbreviates it. The grammatically commoner form, *If A is B, C is D,* is had by substituting a consequent determined by the same ground. Thus, *if the weather* (A) *turns warm* (B), { *the mercury* (C) *rises* (D).
= *it* (A) *expands mercury* (C).

plainly abstract only when its import is general. When its import is particular, the sentence can express the relation *if S, then P* as matter of practical concern, and make question of the existence of *S*. The speaker's attitude towards *S*'s status as fact then gives the distinction between "open" condition, in which it is non-committal, and "rejected" condition, in which it denies—except in supposal as to the future, where denial must weaken into doubt. Since Greek and Latin use differences of mood to suggest the import as general or particular, these distinctions give the following typical varieties of conditional sentence:—

		Past	Present	Future
open	particular	If he *was* right, I *was* wrong. sī aderat, bene erat. εἰ ἔπραξε τοῦτο, καλῶς εἶχεν.	If he {*is* / *be*} right, I *am* wrong. sī adest, bene est. εἰ πράσσει τοῦτο, καλῶς ἔχει.	If he {*wins* / *win*} he *will* return. sī aderit, bene erit. {εἰ πράξει / ἐὰν πράσσῃ} τοῦτο, καλῶς ἕξει.
	general	εἴ τις κλέπτοι, ἐκολάζετο. [If (ever) anyone stole, he (always) got punished.] sī quid dīceret, crēdēbātur.	ἐάν τις κλέπτῃ, κολάζεται. [If ——— steals, he gets punished.] sī hōc dīcās, crēditur.	——— [covered by present.] ———
p. & pr. rejected	*fut.* doubtful	If he *had been* right, I *should* be wrong. sī hōc fecisset, bene fuisset. εἰ ἔπραξε τοῦτο, καλῶς ἂν ἔσχεν.	If he *were* right, I *should*, etc. sī vīviret, verba êius audīrētis. εἰ ἔπρασσε τοῦτο, καλῶς ἂν εἶχεν.	If he *should* win, he *would* return. sī hōc faciat, bene sit. εἰ πράσσοι τοῦτο, καλῶς ἂν ἔχοι.

Suppositions can of course be had in which the status as fact is not rejected or open but accepted. Condition then becomes concession. In analytic speech this modal change can be made by simple stress; thus, *if he is' a don, he's no scholar.* Since condition in one term of a sentence does not suspend its assertion as a whole, concessive statements show more "downrightness" than conditional ones only in their *if*-clauses. As wholes the latter assert a relation between assertions, and are as "downright" as any other statements.

iv. The INTERROGATIVE sentence calls for an assertive word or words from the hearer, and is hence a special case of the imperative. It is of two varieties: (1) Part-questions, as *who spoke? Cain did what to Abel? you went where?* Such questions contain an assertion (as that *somebody* spoke) but one of incomplete content, offering a conceptual blank, such as *who, what, how, quis,* τίς, ποῖος, for the hearer to fill out. (2) Whole-questions, as *do cats eat bats? has Brutus called? are you going?* These offer the complete content of a desired assertion, but put in question its status as fact. Their appeal for a confirming *yes* or *no* is in Greek and Latin pointed by special interjection-like particles: ἦ, ἆρα οὐ, ἆρα μή, *ne, nōnne, num.*

Formally the four types of sentence have each its characteristic particles, word-order, stress, and intonation; but where the context makes a given sentence-value evident, its grammatical formula may be varied for expressive effect. Thus a rhetorical question (*shall Rome lie under one man's sway?*) may have the value of an emphatic denial; a command (*seek, and ye shall find*) may express condition (='if ye seek'). The form of a sentence gives only the grammatical intention as to its kind.

Educational Aims in Sentence-Study. Our account of the mental facts presupposed in syntax leaves us with a question as to its bearing upon sentence-study in the schools. So long as grammar is taken as a mere formal summary to be mastered for correctness in speaking and writing, its approach to sentence-structure will be external, leaving the inner categories pretty much as they occur to common sense. School work in the foreign tongues naturally begins with an aim thus immediately practical, but Greek and Latin claim a value as discipline, and study of the vernacular deserves no place in the class-room at all unless it aims, as J. S. Mill urged, to show how "the forms of language are made to correspond with the universal forms of thought," so that "the structure of every sentence is a lesson in logic." Mill's ideal has not lacked the lip-service of educators. Thus the Committee of Fifteen dwell upon English grammar "as a discipline in subtle analysis, in logical division and classification, in the art of questioning, and in the accomplishment of making exact definitions." Sound analysis and classification, however, such as result from a first-hand survey of the facts of speech, figure very imperfectly in school text-books. Their writers, indeed, excuse their makeshift definitions on the plea that living speech is not to be brought within logical formulas and categories—as if the fact that one's subject-matter is non-logical warranted bad logic in what one says about it. To some extent their confusion can be laid to their having to work with a nomenclature that is not critically valid. This defect alone is enough to defeat their aim to afford a mental training, and should stir them to a hearty support of the movement here and abroad for bringing our grammatical nomenclature into consistency. But it is to be hoped that work of the intensive kind sketched in these chapters will inspire them and the committees directing this movement with a regard for two vital points: (1) that in harmonising the names for like features in different tongues we should not gloss over the seemingly small diversities that make their different genius; (2) that we need not only more consistency in the use of terms but more terms.[1] Speech has its being first of all in facts of utterance, and only at one remove in writing and print; but our means of describing it derive chiefly from the study of written Latin, and so exclusive is

[1] See, for example, Henry Sweet's *New English Grammar*, in which many are improvised.

its prestige that we heedlessly overlook syntactic features of word-order, stress, and intonation, simply because they do not find us prepared with their appropriate labels. Again, familiar as we are with the warning not to describe English constructions by Latin, we are still reduced to this error by our lack of certain terms free from the special *formal* associations of Latin. Even so staple a term as "noun" when applied interchangeably, say, to *city* and *urbs* can make confusion. The Latin for *city* is the notional kernel *urb-*, since the noun suffix *-s* is simply a bit of context showing for *urb-* what is shown for *city* by its position or stress.[1] Elements may not only go unnoted for want of names, but get names that connote too much. The danger of thus sophisticating the data of grammar grows more serious as we pass to speech of an alien type such as Chinese, for it is a frailty of the mind to treat the names of things as a sort of *a priori* evidence of the things themselves.

Where sentence-study begins to be a discipline it calls for sustained work with abstractions somewhat beyond the grasp of young pupils. It should therefore be taken in two short distinct stages, instead of being elaborated through all the grades. The elementary stage may well come early, for the child is already using speech, and can

[1] I have discussed this further in a paper on 'The Rational Study of English Grammar' (*The School Review*, Nov., 1910).

easily be interested in its forms. He has first to discern the judgment-form that gives unity to the sentence, taking its subject and predicate as wholes; to learn the meaning of its relating elements; and to get a practical notion of mood, tense, and the distinctions of direct and reported speech. Even at this stage he should understand the sentence as an organic thought-whole that divides its expression between notional and formative word-rudiments, and not as a mechanical sum of words.

At the high-school stage grammar should take a like organic view of the paragraph, beginning with this as the larger whole that divides its expression between sentence-units. The study of word-forms and word-order here bears especially upon the practice of composition; but as commonly taught its bearing seems too much a matter of afterthought and revision, and not of resourceful *pre*vision. It takes sentences not as plastically forefelt in their relation to contexts, but as things detached, objective, and ready-made. Apart from contexts the pupil can see no use for diverse forms of a sentence that do not appreciably change its content, and he grows to feel that much of his grammatical lore deals with the mere whims and superfluities of speech. Diversities of grammatical form, however, are what afford the nice adjustments by which any given thought becomes amenable to a due sequence and salience within various larger thought-wholes. As differently cast it offers in its changed formatives and re-ordered rhythm fresh structural clues through which it holds to one or another impelling interest. A working command of grammar, therefore, means the ability not merely to take an abstracted sentence and label its notional and relating elements, much less its words, but to take any sentence as it stands in a paragraph and tell *how that choice of elements for it* not only brings its concept-factors into view, but *maintains their relation to that larger whole.* One weakness of an immature writer lies precisely herein, that, seeing his larger design neither steadily nor as a whole, he seems at the mercy of his own sentences. Whatever the wording in which his sentence-thought comes to mind, down it goes on paper, and then stares at him, inert and uncompliant with any further trend. For his trouble the maxims of rhetoric make no provision. "Unity," "just emphasis," "coherence," are terms that presuppose an inner informing principle, and apply only to its manifested results. The inner principle itself is *relevance*: the bearing of all parts of a composition upon its purposive concern as a whole. So long as paragraphs are composed by adding rigid sentence-units one to another they must result in the mechanical stiffness of tesselated work. Truly organic paragraphs begin with a phase of maturation and cleavage within a germ-idea. Their sentences define themselves in each case by a choice between free alternatives both in the notional units, affixes, and particles to be used, and in their disposal—a choice that must spring from the purport of that germ-idea. Grammar then should reinforce rhetoric, not only by noting the varieties of syntactic device, but by showing that behind any sentence-group lies the larger purport, selecting and ordering its syntactic items much as a magnet, passed under a paper of filings, draws all their haphazard bits into one concentric pattern.

Sentence-study in this its further course is high-school philosophy. It can profitably keep in view the diverse speech-material that the pupil meets in his work with foreign languages, and lead him from English grammar, Latin grammar, French grammar, to a conception of general grammar, the study of the linguistic medium of thinking. To the youthful critic any meaning that he finds untractable to his familiar idiom seems unthinkable. Philosophy begins for him when he can free his thought from the letter of its medium, and the first step here is a discernment of the grammatical conditions to which it is variously subject.

In the critical study of the sentence grammar anticipates logic at a fruitful point where it deals with the implication and application of names, and the force of general assertions. It can open the pupil's eyes to the fact that his progress in knowledge takes place largely by improving upon the half-truths of common sense: statements which are true in many but not all their applications. Much wordy debate would be brushed aside if more thinkers had learned in their language-study to recognise the small verbal defects that easily pass unnoticed in generalisation. Knowledge grows by attending to the *application* of statements, but the untrained disputant is continually betrayed into saving their literal truth by turning them into abstract definitions—forgetting that a generalisation has its value between the extremes of an uncriticised half-truth on the one hand, and a truism on the other. An early interest in the function of names will prepare students of the syllogism to see that its criticism is directed upon the complexity of facts as names set them out. Since any name (as '*carbon*') is simply legal tender for a set of judgments (as that 'it burns,' 'it composes diamonds,' etc.), it makes any statement split into a set of statements. A syllogism thus shows the validity of a conclusion (such as '*diamonds burn*') by drawing into view two of its implied statements which our stored-up knowledge confirms as fact, and which disclose it as a particular case of a general rule.[1]

Grammar need not run into logic in order to

[1] The substance of this paragraph is admirably developed in Alfred Sidgwick's *The Use of Words in Reasoning.*

rank as a discipline, but it will maintain itself as such only by giving insight of this kind. Too much has been made in the past of a disciplinary value in its mere drill with inflections, or in the fact that grammatical ideas are abstract. The mind is not to be trained by a routine of mental pulley-weights, for the power to think, like the will to do right, develops best as a by-product of effort directed upon something worth while in itself. When grammar can rest its case on imparting real insight into the rich and subtle medium that it works with, it may regain something of its prestige in the middle age, when it headed the roll of the Seven Liberal Arts.

INDEX

www.ingramcontent.com/pod-product-compliance
Lightning Source LLC
LaVergne TN
LVHW011214110826
845150LV00006B/1427

* 9 7 8 1 4 2 5 5 7 2 3 9 6 *